I0037729

'A must-read for anyone wanting to understand, educate and empower people around them to be more inclusive in all realms of diversity, equity and inclusion.'
Estelle Jackson, Global Lead for Diversity, Equity and Inclusion, eBay

'Wow! What an interesting read – authentic and backed by insights and useful facts on the full suite of why an organization should harness neurodiversity. This book is peppered with many hints and tips throughout that are impossible to skip!'
Nimisha Overton, Diversity, Equity and Inclusion Lead EMEA, Canon

'Truly one of a kind. Thomas Duncan Bell's story is so powerful in helping to educate, erase the stigma linked to neurodivergence, and contribute to a positive change within organizations and society. Essential reading!'
Kirsty McLean, Head of Wellbeing, Nomura

'The time is now for a more inclusive definition of success, based on holistic health and wellbeing. Thomas Duncan Bell's book goes deep into the root of the problem. With unique testimonials and work-place wellbeing hacks, there is something here for everyone.'
Karen Rivoire, Global Talent Officer, IKEA

'Totally relatable content! Thomas Duncan Bell not only understands neurodiversity and our need as a society to get better, but he provides tools to help you hone, harness and execute your true values as a business.'
Jane O'Mahoney, Deputy Director of Workplace Transformation, House of Commons

'I was hooked from the first page. Thomas Duncan Bell not only brings the subject of neurodiversity in business to life but does so with honesty and compassion. I highly recommend this to any HR or H&S lead in today's workforce – in fact, to any business leader! The insights in this book are a true gift.'
Stephen Haynes, Director of Wellbeing, British Safety Council

'Thomas Duncan Bell fundamentally flips the narrative on neurodiversity. This book will help you unlock the untapped potential that exists in your organization today. An empowering read for neurodivergent people and a critical read for business leaders everywhere.'
Catherine Ritchie, Senior Wellbeing and Experience Manager

Spectrum of Success

How embracing neurodiversity can revolutionize your business

Thomas Duncan Bell

KoganPage

First published in Great Britain and the United States in 2025 by Kogan Page Limited

2nd Floor, 45 Gee Street
London
EC1V 3RS
United Kingdom

8 W 38th Street, Suite 902
New York, NY 10018
USA

www.koganpage.com

Kogan Page books are printed on paper from sustainable forests.

© Thomas Duncan Bell, 2025

ISBNs
Hardback   978 1 3986 1664 6
Paperback   978 1 3986 1662 2
Ebook   978 1 3986 1663 9

British Library Cataloguing-in-Publication Data
A CIP record for this book is available from the British Library.

Library of Congress Cataloging-in-Publication Data
Names: Bell, Thomas Duncan, author.
Title: Spectrum of success : how embracing neurodiversity can revolutionize your business / Thomas Duncan Bell.
Description: London ; New York, NY : Kogan Page Inc., 2025. | Includes bibliographical references and index.
Identifiers: LCCN 2024031632 (print) | LCCN 2024031633 (ebook) | ISBN 9781398616622 (paperback) | ISBN 9781398616646 (hardback) | ISBN 9781398616639 (ebook)
Subjects: LCSH: Diversity in the workplace. | Neurodivergent people–Employment. | Creative thinking. | Organizational effectiveness.
Classification: LCC HF5549.5.M5 B454 2025 (print) | LCC HF5549.5.M5 (ebook) | DDC 658.3008–dc23/eng/20240709
LC record available at https://lccn.loc.gov/2024031632
LC ebook record available at https://lccn.loc.gov/2024031633

Typeset by Integra Software Services, Pondicherry
Print production managed by Jellyfish
Printed and bound by CPI Group (UK) Ltd, Croydon CR0 4YY

CONTENTS

FOREWORD

Thomas Duncan Bell, also known as The Bipolar Businessman, is a remarkable individual who has defied societal norms and stigma surrounding mental health to become a successful entrepreneur, speaker and mental health advocate. His journey not only exemplifies resilience in the face of mental health challenges but also underscores the potential for individuals with bipolar disorder, attention deficit hyperactivity disorder (ADHD) and other neurodivergent traits to thrive in the professional world. Let me give you a little more insight into Thomas Duncan Bell's unique story, highlighting the strengths associated with his neurodiversity that have contributed to his success.

Firstly, individuals with bipolar disorder and ADHD often experience heightened creativity during manic or hypomanic phases. Thomas has harnessed this creative energy to his advantage, using it to develop innovative ideas and solutions within his business ventures over two decades. His ability to think outside the box and approach challenges with a fresh perspective has been a driving force in his success.

But, while the unpredictable nature of bipolar disorder and ADHD can present challenges in maintaining consistent work patterns, individuals like Thomas often develop remarkable resilience and determination in navigating the highs and lows of their condition. And Thomas clearly has an unparalleled level of resilience that has enabled him to overcome a wide variety of extreme obstacles and persist in his entrepreneurial pursuits where many would have fallen flat on their face or bowed out early.

Bipolar and ADHD individuals often experience periods of hyperfocus and heightened productivity during manic phases. Thomas has also successfully channelled these bursts of energy into his work, allowing him to achieve significant milestones during these periods and catapult him into becoming one of the most respected mental health speakers in the UK today, if not on a global level.

Having first-hand experience with the challenges of bipolar disorder and ADHD, as well as suffering more than anyone deserves to, for various reasons, throughout the course of his life Thomas has cultivated within a deep sense of empathy and emotional intelligence. This heightened understanding of emotional nuances allows him to connect with others on a profound level, both in his professional endeavours and as a mental health advocate, and you really can't teach that, it's simply authentic at its core.

What's also interesting about people with neurodivergent traits similar to Thomas is that they often exhibit a higher propensity for risk-taking, especially during manic phases, but Thomas's willingness to take more assertive and calculated risks has been instrumental in his entrepreneurial journey, which sees him embracing uncertainty and leveraging risk as an opportunity for growth, and that's set him apart in the business world.

His journey as The Bipolar Businessman has necessitated effective communication about mental health via millions of people all over the planet. His ability to articulate his experiences with bipolar disorder, among other issues, has not only shattered stigma but has also contributed to a broader conversation about mental health in the workplace that takes most experts in the field far longer to navigate. Effective communication skills are a valuable asset in leadership and advocacy roles and Thomas sets himself apart, which I believe is in part due not only to his charisma, but also to his neurodivergence.

What's more is that the challenges associated with bipolar disorder and ADHD often lead individuals to adopt a holistic approach to their overall wellbeing, so as he educates businesses, teams and leaders, Thomas emphasizes the importance of mental health, self-care and a balanced lifestyle, and this holistic perspective has not only contributed to his personal resilience but has also influenced his approach to business and leadership, and we certainly need more of that!

While the strengths associated with bipolar disorder can contribute to success, it is crucial to acknowledge the challenges and complexities that individuals like Thomas may face. These conditions require ongoing management and the interplay between the highs and lows can pose unique difficulties in maintaining consistent work patterns, but when it comes to your staff the importance of a strong support system, access to mental health resources and open communication about one's condition cannot be overstated.

Thomas's journey as The Bipolar Businessman is a testament to the potential for individuals with neurodiversity not only to succeed but also to thrive in their professional lives. By embracing the strengths associated with the condition, such as heightened creativity, resilience and effective communication skills, Thomas has become a trailblazer in both the business and mental health advocacy realms. His story challenges preconceived notions about mental health in the workplace and highlights the importance of fostering environments that promote understanding, acceptance and support for individuals with bipolar disorder, ADHD and other mental health conditions.

Thomas's journey stands as an inspiration for others facing similar challenges, demonstrating that one's unique mental health journey can be a source of strength and empowerment. And The Bipolar Businessman's success story invites us to reconsider how we perceive mental health in the professional world. By recognizing and celebrating the strengths associated with neurodiversity, we can create workplaces that embrace diversity, foster resilience and promote the holistic wellbeing of all individuals, contributing to a more compassionate and inclusive society. I am glad to know him and proud to call him a friend.

Geoff McDonald
Former Global Vice President of HR and Marketing, Unilever

Introduction

As human beings, we tend to focus only on the after-effect. We tend to want to put a 'Band-Aid' – a temporary solution – on the issue after the wound has been opened, but we rarely look at where that wound came from or how to prevent that issue from happening again. And this is where we fall down. It's not just where our society falls down, it's also why businesses across the world fail those working among their ranks on a daily basis, particularly those who are neurodiverse.

We are too ready, when it comes to mental health, to try to fix the problem after the fact and never to rectify or better understand the habits that cause friction, or to retain an employee before they hand in their resignation.

A Chartered Institute of Personnel and Development survey found that a fifth of neurodivergent individuals report to have suffered prejudice in the workplace and that many companies just don't focus enough on neurodiversity and neuro-inclusion. Thirty-three per cent of the people surveyed in this report felt that the way they had been treated had had a negative impact on their mental health and overall mental wellbeing; and 21 per cent said that a poor level of support and lack of understanding had had a detrimental effect on their ability to work and perform the role they were hired for.[1]

Deloitte studies have clearly shown that, when nurtured, neurodivergent individuals can in fact be 30 per cent more effective in their roles than the average neurotypical individual. So, surely that makes a case for cultivation and understanding as well as empathy and proactive measures for support in every workplace, especially if 20 per cent of your staff are likely to be neurodivergent.[2]

I never wanted to be a businessman, and I spent most of my life wanting to know what the point was. My reason for living. Why we are here. I felt jaded by the start I got, living in a pressure-cooker environment with two gay parents who couldn't come out and live their lives as they should have because it wasn't acceptable at the time for them to be who they wanted to be. There was too much prejudice in the world. And this difficult start led me to a lifetime of introspection, regardless of my ability to try to heal the issues it caused within.

When you stop putting pressure on yourself, when you stop judging yourself, when you stop measuring yourself against how a prescriptive society defines you, then you free yourself.

When we first attend school, we are trained how to think and how to form an opinion. We are taught how to pass our exams and eventually we might head to university, with a loan that many of us spend our lifetime paying off. Before we know it, we are thrust into the world of work, fighting to clear our debt and earn a living so that we can buy a house and maybe build a family and have kids.

And so, it goes around, this cycle of life, until it is broken by the activist within us.

But my journey has been a bit different. I'm on the bipolar spectrum, with a side order of attention deficit hyperactivity disorder (ADHD), post-traumatic stress disorder (PTSD), dyslexia and dyspraxia. I'm literally a veritable smorgasbord of certifiable madness, but I chose to channel what I have and what I've lived through in order to save or improve a life where I can.

I think it's important to mention that, as with any minority group, I have a mission in writing this book. That fundamentally comes down to the fact that I have been consistently judged throughout my career for the way that I operate, some of which comes down to my personality and some of which comes down to my neurodiversity. However, I ultimately never felt comfortable talking about my diagnosis with employers in the past, and it's even been challenging in recently years to work with people or gain trust, despite my 20 years of experience, simply because I wear my diagnosis on my sleeve.

It's a consistent issue I see in businesses with human resources (HR) and leaders sidelining or not focusing on neurodiversity, so this book will offer some fundamental insights and strategies that will allow any business to actively change their approach to neurodiversity in a way that will create impact and inclusion.

The book is in three parts:

- **Part One – Understanding neurodiversity:** This section establishes some fundamental knowledge on the wider context of various mental health diagnoses that can be classified as neurodiverse and delves into some of the facts, myths and intricacies of neurodiversity within the wider context of diversity, equity, inclusion and wellbeing strategies. It offers insights both for business leaders looking to transform their business and for individuals looking to develop a better understanding of neurodiversity and how it might relate to themselves.

- **Part Two – Empowering your business:** This section offers frameworks that will show you how to really harness neurodivergent staff and channel them towards success. It also explores the benefits of neurodivergent leaders and how to cultivate neurodiverse leaders proactively, as well as recruit the right neurodiverse talent, and a whole host of additional information. There are also insights into how to create an inclusive culture, and most of this section of the book is about providing you with insights, strategies and step-by-step options for creating sustainable change.

- **Part Three – Establishing sustainable change:** By this stage you will understand the importance of neurodiversity and will be armed with some strategies. This section will show you how to transform that knowledge into practical and lasting change, exploring the dynamics and frameworks that you can bring into play to actually make a difference without burning your budget.

This book will not only help you gain insight and understanding into the field of neurodiversity, it will also inspire you along the way and give you productive and proactive tips that will serve you well as you build some robust foundations for your business. If you're an individual looking for more introspection and clarity, it will help you start to explore who you are.

Notes

1 J Rowsell. Fifth of neurodivergent workers have experienced workplace discrimination, report finds, *People Management*, 20 February 2024. www.peoplemanagement.co.uk/article/1862106/fifth-neurodivergent-workers-experienced-workplace-discrimination-report-finds (archived at https://perma.cc/9Z3P-DV3Y)

2 M Mahto, S Hogan and B Snidderman. A rising tide lifts all boats, Deloitte Insights, 18 January 2024. www2.deloitte.com/us/en/insights/topics/talent/neurodiversity-in-the-workplace.html (archived at https://perma.cc/HU37-WEUZ)

PART ONE

Understanding neurodiversity

1

Understanding the fundamentals

On a fundamental level, embracing my neurodiversity has set me on a pathway to achieving success in life. That doesn't mean I'm a multi-millionaire, or that everyone I meet will immediately adore me. What it does mean is that I have achieved a greater sense of self, a deeper and wider breadth of knowledge as to who I am as an individual, who I want to be and what values I most hold dear. And, with that, I am far more effective as a human being when it comes to tackling the slings and arrows that are set to thwart our progression day-to-day, as people try to hold me back or cast aspersions as to who they 'think' I am, based on a preconceived notion of diagnosis, or a misunderstanding of my energy or personality.

What is neurodiversity?

The very definition of neurodiversity is that it's a viewpoint that our individual brain differences are normal, rather than deficits. Neurodivergent people experience, interact with and interpret the world in unique ways, as opposed to neurotypical individuals. This base line concept can help reduce stigma around learning and thinking differences and it is this definition that should be held to whenever the fundamentals around neurodiversity are considered.

Neurodiversity is a concept that challenges traditional views of neurological differences, advocating for the acceptance and celebration of diverse neurological conditions and abilities. Coined by

Australian sociologist Judy Singer in the late 1990s, the term emphasizes the idea that neurological differences, such as autism, ADHD, dyslexia and others, are natural variations of the human brain rather than deviations from the 'norm'.[1]

Throughout this book I will delve into the essence of neurodiversity, its impact on individuals and society, and the reasons why embracing neurodiversity can pave the way for success in various aspects of life, whether that be for individuals, or for the businesses who should focus attention on cultivating a workforce that thinks and operates a little differently.

Current definitions of 'disorders' that fall within the neurodiverse spectrum include:

- **Autism spectrum disorders (ASD):** Autism is a neurodevelopmental disorder characterized by differences in social interaction, communication and behaviour. (Approximately 1 per cent of people.)[2]
- **Attention deficit hyperactivity disorder (ADHD):** ADHD is a neurodevelopmental disorder that affects a person's ability to pay attention, control impulsive behaviours and regulate activity levels. (Approximately 2–7 per cent of people.)[3]
- **Dyslexia:** Dyslexia is a learning disorder that affects reading, spelling and writing abilities, often characterized by difficulties with phonological processing. (Approximately 5–10 per cent of people.)[4]
- **Dyspraxia (developmental coordination disorder):** Dyspraxia involves difficulties with motor coordination, and planning and executing physical tasks. (Approximately 5–6 per cent of people.)[5]
- **Intellectual disabilities:** Conditions characterized by limitations in intellectual functioning and adaptive behaviour, affecting everyday social and practical skills. (Approximately 1–3 per cent of people.)[6]
- **Tourette's syndrome:** Tourette's syndrome involves repetitive, involuntary movements and vocalizations called tics. (Approximately 0.5–1 per cent of people.)[7]

- **Obsessive-compulsive disorder (OCD):** While traditionally viewed as an anxiety disorder, some consider OCD as part of the neurodiversity spectrum due to its neurological components. (Approximately 1–2 per cent of people.)[8]
- **Schizophrenia and other psychotic disorders:** Some discussions include conditions like schizophrenia within the neurodiversity framework, emphasizing the diversity of cognitive experiences. (Approximately 0.3–0.7 per cent of people.)[9]
- **Dyscalculia:** A specific learning disorder that affects an individual's ability to understand and work with numbers and mathematical concepts. (Approximately 6 per cent of people.)[10]
- **Epilepsy:** A neurological disorder characterized by recurrent, unprovoked seizures. Seizures are sudden, excessive electrical discharges in the brain that can manifest in various ways, affecting behaviour, consciousness or motor functions. (Approximately 0.5–1 per cent of people.)[11]

In addition to the above, I would also consider the following to be neurodivergent disorders:

- **Bipolar disorder:** Formerly known as manic-depressive illness, this is a mood disorder characterized by extreme mood swings, including episodes of mania (elevated mood, increased energy) and depression (low mood, loss of interest or pleasure). (Approximately 4.4 per cent of people.)[12]
- **Borderline personality disorder (BPD):** A mental health condition characterized by pervasive patterns of emotional instability, impulsivity, intense and tumultuous relationships, identity disturbance and a persistent fear of abandonment. (Approximately 1–2 per cent of people.)[13]

What separates bipolar disorder and borderline personality disorder from being categorized as obvious neurodivergent disorders, in my eyes, is that there's more evidence to suggest that bipolar and BPD are not genetically established mental health disorders, but rather learned behaviours, stemming from the environmental development of the individuals who struggle with these. However, the skills and attributes that come off the back of these additional two diagnoses are still akin to the attributes that many people with other neurodiverse diagnoses will benefit from, as much as some of the negative aspects surrounding bipolar and BPD may have an extreme impact on the individuals.[14]

So, if I were a company looking to establish a foundation to support and look after my neurodiverse staff, then I would consider all of the 12 types listed above, as opposed to limiting the definition to those that seem more obvious to the HR generalist.

The business advantages of embracing neurodiversity

At its core, neurodiversity recognizes and appreciates the spectrum of neurological variations present in the human population. Just as biodiversity is crucial for the health and resilience of ecosystems, neurodiversity contributes to the richness and adaptability of the human experience. The neurodiversity paradigm challenges the prevailing medical model that pathologizes neurological differences and aims to create a more inclusive and accepting society.

Each condition brings unique strengths, challenges and perspectives to the table. Rather than viewing these differences as deficits, the neurodiversity movement asserts that society should value and accommodate neurodivergent individuals, recognizing their potential contributions on a wider level.

It's so easy to rule people out because of a preconceived notion that they are broken, or that they exhibit unwanted traits. God knows, I have been sidelined for being over-energetic, loud or too open with my honest thoughts surrounding project decisions or a business's approach. On many occasions I've been abused or unfairly treated because of how I operate off the back of my neurodiversity. To many, my methods or approach to business may seem unorthodox, but those who have got behind me and supported what I bring to the table have seen the impact that I can have, whether that results in increased revenue or new innovative ideas. Ultimately, it shouldn't matter if an approach is unorthodox (as long as it's not disruptive or detrimental to others) – if it ends with clear results then businesses should encourage neurodiverse employees to use their own methods to achieve incredible things.

One good example from my personal journey was during a contracted role running business development for a business process management company, whom you might have thought would be interested in improved processes and, like any good tech company, some increased incremental revenue.

I was tasked with finding and delivering £1 million of incremental revenue through new customers per annum. This meant sourcing contacts from cold, engaging with them and selling them software and service provision in the region of £50,000–£250,000 as a minimum contract value. No problem. I was a seasoned sales professional at this point, I knew how to break down a tech proposition and develop solid relationships, so very quickly I was able to develop a pipeline of nearly £6 million in incremental revenue because my process for sourcing, engaging and account managing prospective customers was systematic. With my open and charismatic approach to building relationships, I'd clearly shown that if the company utilized my process across all the business development folks throughout the US, Europe, Middle East and Africa, then the company would inevitably dwarf its competition.

Now, any innovative C-suite with an eye for talent and a penchant for more money would think that they'd have hoisted me onto their shoulders and paraded me around the boardroom. However, having explained to my managers about my increased ability to convert at 600 per cent my annual target, I was told that the internal processes globally would remain the same, because that's just how marketing do things. I wasn't sold on this. I decided to take this up the food chain. So, I hastily set aside some time with the global vice-president (VP) of sales, who thought my idea was solid and sustainable, and he said that he would take it to the next board meeting and discuss it with all senior directors, including the global VP of marketing, whose budget funded my role. I felt heard and validated for my ambition and tenacity.

I heard nothing back. So, as a budding entrepreneur who couldn't understand why a company wouldn't want to earn more money, I chased my global VP of sales once again. But the feedback was that the global VP of marketing had been quite embarrassed that a young upstart had undermined their conservative approach to growth and that my ideas would not be taken forward to evolve the business development process. Within weeks, a new sales director was brought in and his first order of business was to inform me that marketing no longer had a budget to invest in my role and I was subsequently ushered out of the business, having over-achieved in every context. This is why employees are so scared to innovate, because it never comes down to how effective you are – it comes down to whose nose you put out of joint along the way. When money or status are involved, people will drag you into the dirt to ensure their upward trajectory stays on course.

One of the primary advantages of embracing neurodiversity is the enhancement of cognitive diversity within groups and communities. Neurodivergent individuals very often possess unique cognitive strengths, such as heightened pattern recognition; they are also unique in their ability to manage attention to detail and diverse innovative or creative thinking. These diverse cognitive styles contribute to more comprehensive problem-solving approaches, fostering creativity and resilience in the face of complex challenges. Personally, I've found this valuable through my ability to rethink a problem, but every neurodiverse person has their own unique abilities and advantages.[15]

It may sound mundane to the average person, but many neurodiverse individuals get more momentum out of the internal compass that leads them than they do out of any 'pay day' they might receive off the back of doing good work. The ethics have always been what drove me as an individual, the humanity of a relationship, a deal, a partnership. We are more emotionally attached to delivering to a high standard in the context of vocation and our wider lives and that can often lead to wearing our heart on our sleeve or being taken advantage of off the back of it. There are exceptions to this rule, when neurodiverse people are looked after and appreciated for their innovation and initiative, but those moments may be few and far between. More business leaders need to recognize the power of a neurodiverse individual when you set them in the right direction or afford them freedom to innovate and evolve.

Discussing neurodivergent traits and needs

As an individual you should be mindful of choosing the appropriate time and setting when you think about discussing your neurodivergent traits and/or needs. It's important to consider what type of people you might be sharing your needs with, so that you know they are open and collaborative. Try to be mindful of choosing somewhere you feel safe to engage, a space where you're comfortable and relaxed. And always remember that timing is an important factor, because if the person you are sharing your thoughts with doesn't have the capacity to have a meaningful conversation surrounding your experience and needs, then you will never get the best momentum out of being brave enough to engage on the subject.

We should also be framing the conversation in a positive light and considering our attributes, because if we highlight our strengths and those diverse insights that only come easy to the neurodivergent community, then we as individuals can help shift the balance in the discussion towards an outcome that's more pragmatic and empowers us and the individual we let in. This also ensures a wider level of understanding. If you in turn focus on your unique abilities, then you add weight through awareness of what's possible for you, if nurtured, vs other neurotypical individuals. If everyone begins by focusing on neurodivergence as an asset, you can challenge negative or ill-conceived stereotypes and help those around you see more of the potential throughout our community.

Another fundamental when looking at your personal limitations or the limitations of individuals around you, is to ensure that the discussion is circumstantially accurate. It's really paramount to acknowledge shortcomings you are challenged by due to your neurodivergence, but only by providing understandable circumstances can we truly help others in their consideration and education surrounding how these issues can be supported, to get the best outcome for you. If you think about strategies that have helped you become more effective, it's easier for others to support your progress, so throw out some problems and coping strategies or solutions – don't just focus on the negative. In offering neurotypical peers transparency into how you have adapted to get the best from yourself then you will better help them understand how you manage your needs and you effectively showcase how resilient and adaptive you are evidentially, and that makes for a compelling argument for support and understanding.

Always make it personal, because then people become more understanding of where you are when it comes to finding your path. They also understand better that it's a progression over time, an evolution of self, and that you may not fully understand or be aware of what your needs are. However, you must be mindful to also think about whether you feel comfortable talking about these things, and the potential impact of these discussions when you share that part of yourself. It may be helpful if you let someone in a little bit at a time, especially if you start talking to people you trust within your environment who are more likely to be open or supportive and can also give you ideas and insights as to how best to open up the conversation on a wider level to aid your development as an individual or within a company role. If you afford yourself the ability to be vulnerable with someone and build some trust, you can see how they respond and decide how much more of yourself you want to share over time. If you empower your neurodivergent employees and give them the support, safety and freedom to harness their innate skillset then they will feel empowered, they will be far more productive for you, and this will inevitably earn your business more money or save your business time. It simply makes sense to invest in finding out what your neurodiverse staff contingent are capable of when they're flying your banner with the freedom to indulge themselves a little in bringing about change for the greater good of the business.

Overcoming friction and resistance

One potential issue for neurodiverse employees is that their unconventional methods can cause friction in the organization (particularly when these methods result in huge success!). I have experienced this myself, when my ability to increase revenue and cultivate more business resulted in frustration from other departments, with the view that my success had shone a light on the inefficiency of their methods.

I have run my own businesses since I was 20 years old, so I know what it's like to earn money and then realize that you've been wasting lots of money on the wrong things. Through our unique perspectives, neurodiverse employees have the superpower of finding ways to improve businesses and build connections at little or no cost.

I've always preferred to create engaging ways to talk to the customers or followers of a given brand that adds value for all parties. When companies come together because of shared values and utilize each other's assets by means of creating engaging content and initiatives, those consumers or clients are far more likely to hold value for the brands in question because they see your human value – they see what you're all about.

While I was working with Pepe Jeans Group we ran an initiative that was looking at promoting more sustainable and eco-led fashion and we bolstered that message with a competition to engage the customers of a major mobile telephone network, with an approach that might pique their interest and have individuals sharing this message to promote our company values. Now, the point was not to create sales but to create awareness for the mission and to show people what the brand was all about. Neither company paid the other any money, but off the back of the creativity and the messaging we had 250,000 people get involved in that campaign. And that's a lot of eyes on a message that makes you think about your impact on the planet. So, in innovating and being creative with partner assets you can more widely evoke a positive brand perception and build trust with those who follow you, far faster than if you stick a dirty discount on the website or sling out some daily deals.

Studies have shown that neurodivergent individuals, particularly those with conditions like autism, can excel in fields that require specialized skills, such as mathematics, engineering and technology. By integrating neurodiverse perspectives, teams can create a more holistic understanding of problems and develop innovative solutions that might not have been apparent through conventional approaches. In addition, neurodivergent individuals often exhibit unconventional thinking patterns and a heightened capacity for creativity. In industries that thrive on innovation, such as technology and design, neurodiversity can be a valuable asset. The ability to see the world from different angles and approach problems from unconventional perspectives can lead to breakthrough ideas and solutions.

Companies like Microsoft, SAP and Ernst & Young have recognized the advantages of neurodiversity and actively seek to hire neurodivergent individuals. These organizations understand that a diverse workforce that includes neurodiverse talent fosters a culture of creativity and innovation, ultimately driving the company's success.[16]

One of the most beautiful aspects of being neurodivergent is that, because individuals often experience the world in such unique ways, it can lead to heightened empathy and social awareness. Understanding and appreciating diverse perspectives is essential in building inclusive communities and workplaces, so by embracing neurodiversity society can create environments that value differences and foster a sense of belonging for all individuals, regardless of their neurological makeup.

In addition, the neurodivergent, particularly those with conditions like autism, may possess a deep sense of justice and fairness. This heightened sense of morality can contribute to the creation of more ethical and socially responsible communities, as neurodivergent individuals advocate for inclusivity and social justice. And this is something that I have always personally pride myself on.

Once you sacrifice your ethics in business, it becomes easier to repeat the pattern. Once you sell someone up the river for some quick money, you can never go back. And to me that's always been something that I hold paramount. I have been screwed over many times in my last 20 years in business, primarily because I'm too open and I wear my heart on my sleeve. However, I've never taken advantage of anyone for the sake of financial or egoistic award.

However, going through challenging circumstances and being used and abused throughout my business career, I was lucky once again, because living with neurodivergent conditions often requires individuals to develop resilience and adaptability. Neurodivergent individuals frequently face societal challenges, including stigma, discrimination and a lack of understanding, but overcoming these obstacles can instil a strong sense of resilience and determination, qualities that are valuable in navigating the complexities of life and work.

Neurodivergent individuals, with their unique perspectives and coping mechanisms, can offer valuable insights on navigating change and uncertainty, contributing to the overall resilience of communities and organizations. Do you think that the guy who was bullied all his life is weaker? Because, while his anxiety may be more prevalent than usual, he's far more likely to get the job done when pressure comes calling, and that's a person you want on your team when a tender comes near to close.

Social justice and neurodiversity

Embracing neurodiversity goes beyond recognizing the benefits of diversity in individual success; it is also a social justice movement. The neurodiversity paradigm challenges the societal norms that pathologize and marginalize neurodivergent individuals. By advocating for equal opportunities, accommodation and acceptance, the neurodiversity movement aims to create a more just and inclusive society as a whole.

Promoting neurodiversity aligns with broader efforts to dismantle ableism (the discrimination and social prejudice against people with disabilities). Just as other diversity and inclusion movements have worked towards dismantling racism, sexism and other forms of discrimination, the neurodiversity movement strives to eliminate the stigma associated with neurological differences.

While Chapter 3 will dispel a few myths surrounding the subject, I think it's important to mention early on that, while the benefits of neurodiversity are substantial, there are challenges and misconceptions that persist in society. Stigma, lack of awareness and insufficient support systems can hinder the full realization of neurodiverse individuals' potential. Education and advocacy play crucial roles in dispelling myths and promoting a more inclusive understanding of neurodiversity.

Despite increasing awareness, neurodivergent individuals often face stigma and stereotyping. Misconceptions about certain conditions, such as autism, can perpetuate harmful stereotypes that undermine the abilities and potential of those who are neurodiverse. This means that early-stage education and awareness campaigns are essential in challenging these stereotypes and fostering a more accurate and inclusive understanding of neurodiversity.

One of the services my business offers is a course called 'Legitimate Leadership', a clinically validated leadership training programme where I teach managers and directors how to become more authentic, adaptable and compassionate. However, gaining C-suite approval for this type of activity is often challenging. When I started campaigning for better mental health in business and sharing my story, I proactively labelled myself as 'The Bipolar Businessman', because I thought it would be easier to share my message and heal others. However, when you wear this sort of diagnosis on your sleeve people sometimes expect that you might turn up in their office and just flip out at random, like you're a bomb waiting to go off… As soon as I labelled myself as 'bipolar', my 20 years of experience working with hundreds of businesses and thousands of individuals around the world suddenly became irrelevant in some people's eyes. My credibility and tenure were swept aside based on a misjudged societal preconception or a dictionary diagnosis for something that is absolutely impossible to clearly describe, because so much of the nuance surrounding this diagnosis is based on the situational development of individuals as they grow up and experience life. Ultimately, I could easily remove this title and make life easier for myself, but I won't, because why should I? The issue lies with those who make snap judgements based on a diagnosis, thinking that it solely defines how I operate and points to dysfunctional and disruptive behaviour, rather than an innovative and creative approach to business.

In many educational and workplace settings there is a significant lack of support systems tailored to the needs of neurodivergent individuals. Accommodations, such as flexible work schedules, sensory-friendly environments and communication support, are often overlooked. Creating inclusive environments requires proactive efforts to provide the necessary resources and support for neurodivergent individuals to thrive, and to achieve that, advocacy and education are critical components of the neurodiversity movement.

Promoting awareness

Promoting awareness and understanding of neurodivergent conditions can help dispel myths and challenge preconceived notions. Efforts to integrate neurodiversity into educational curricula and workplace diversity initiatives contribute to a more inclusive society.

It is also essential to recognize the intersectionality of neurodiversity with other aspects of diversity, such as race, gender and socioeconomic status. Neurodivergent individuals may experience compounded challenges when navigating multiple layers of identity. Intersectional approaches to neurodiversity advocacy acknowledge and address these complexities, fostering a more inclusive and equitable movement.

So, let's look at embracing some of the practical implications for individuals seeking success in various aspects of life. Whether in education, employment or personal development, neurodivergent individuals can harness their unique strengths to overcome challenges and achieve their goals.

Education

In the realm of education, understanding and accommodating diverse learning styles is essential. Neurodivergent students may excel in areas such as visual thinking, hands-on learning or specialized subjects. By recognizing and supporting these individual strengths, educators can create inclusive learning environments that cater to the diverse needs of students.[17]

Furthermore, the neurodivergent often exhibit a passion for specific subjects or activities. Nurturing these interests can lead to deep expertise and success in specialized fields. So, tailoring educational experiences to accommodate diverse learning styles and interests benefits not only neurodivergent individuals but the entire learning community.

The workplace

But this brings us back to the office. Because the workplace is a domain where the advantages of neurodiversity are starting to be increasingly recognized. Employers are starting to understand that a neurodiverse workforce brings a wealth of talents and perspectives that will contribute to organizational success. Those companies that are genuinely committed to diversity and inclusion proactively seek neurodivergent talent, understanding that varied cognitive styles foster innovation and creativity, so for neurodivergent individuals entering the workforce, seeking employers with inclusive policies and support structures is crucial. Additionally, embracing one's neurodivergent identity and advocating for necessary accommodations can create a more positive and supportive work environment.

ENTREPRENEURSHIP AND NEURODIVERGENCE: ELON MUSK

One aspect that often goes unnoticed, unless you hear people contextualize the success of neurodiverse individuals like Richard Branson and Elon Musk in the context of entrepreneurship and innovation, is that the entrepreneurial landscape provides neurodivergent people with unique opportunities to leverage their creative thinking and problem-solving skills. Many successful entrepreneurs, including those with conditions like ADHD or autism, attribute their success to their neurodivergent perspectives.

As an example, Elon Musk, the visionary entrepreneur and CEO known for founding companies such as Tesla, SpaceX, Neuralink and The Boring

Company, has captured the world's attention with his ambitious goals and transformative impact on various industries. In May 2021 Musk publicly revealed that he has Asperger's syndrome, a form of autism spectrum disorder.[18]

Here is my exploration into why Elon Musk's Asperger's may have contributed to his success. In my eyes, it comes down to examining the unique traits associated with his condition and how they intersect with his entrepreneurial journey:

- **Intense focus and specialization:** Individuals with Asperger's often exhibit intense focus and dedication to specific areas of interest. Musk's success can be attributed, in part, to his remarkable ability to concentrate deeply on complex technical and engineering challenges. This focus has allowed him to push the boundaries of innovation in fields such as electric vehicles, space exploration and renewable energy.

- **Exceptional problem-solving skills:** Asperger's syndrome is associated with strong analytical and problem-solving skills. Musk's ventures, from developing electric cars to creating reusable rockets, are marked by his ability to approach complex problems with a systematic and innovative mindset. This skill set has been crucial in overcoming hurdles that would deter others.

- **Unconventional thinking and creativity:** Neurodivergent individuals often exhibit unconventional thinking and creativity, unbound by traditional norms. Musk's audacious goals, such as colonizing Mars and creating high-speed underground transportation, reflect a willingness to explore unconventional solutions. This ability to think beyond the conventional has fuelled his success and disrupted industries.

- **Resilience and perseverance:** Asperger's syndrome can sometimes be associated with challenges in social interactions and communication. Musk's resilience and perseverance in the face of adversity have been evident throughout his career. Whether overcoming technical setbacks or navigating complex business landscapes, Musk's determination has played a pivotal role in his success.

- **High level of autonomy:** Neurodivergent individuals often thrive in environments that allow for a high level of autonomy. Musk's leadership style, characterized by a hands-on approach and a deep involvement in technical details, aligns with the desire for autonomy commonly associated with Asperger's. This hands-on engagement has been a driving force behind the success of his ventures.

- **Hyperfocus and work ethic:** Hyperfocus, a common trait in individuals with Asperger's, refers to an intense concentration on a specific task or interest. Musk's legendary work ethic and ability to immerse himself in his projects align with this trait. This intense focus has been a contributing factor in the rapid progress and achievements of his companies.

- **Risk-taking propensity:** Asperger's syndrome can be linked to a reduced sensitivity to social norms and expectations, contributing to a higher risk-taking propensity. Musk's willingness to take bold risks, such as investing personal funds into SpaceX and Tesla during critical junctures, reflects this trait. His calculated risks have often resulted in groundbreaking successes.

- **Innovative vision and long-term thinking:** Neurodivergent individuals may exhibit an innovative vision and a capacity for long-term thinking. I mentioned Musk's ambitious goals, including the colonization of Mars and the pursuit of sustainable energy solutions, and these also showcase a commitment to addressing global challenges with a futuristic perspective. This visionary outlook sets him apart in the business world.

While there are aspects of Asperger's syndrome that may contribute to Musk's success, it is essential to acknowledge the challenges associated with the condition. Social communication difficulties, sensitivity to sensory stimuli and potential struggles with teamwork and collaboration can pose hurdles in professional and personal contexts. Musk himself has acknowledged the impact of Asperger's on his social interactions stating, 'I don't always have a lot of intonation or variation in how I speak... which I'm told makes for great comedy.' Furthermore, it is crucial to avoid generalizations and recognize the individuality of experiences within the neurodivergent community. Not every person with Asperger's will share the same traits or strengths, and success is influenced by a myriad of factors beyond neurodiversity.[19]

Musk's impact extends beyond his individual experiences with Asperger's, emphasizing the importance of fostering inclusive environments that celebrate neurodiversity. By recognizing and leveraging the unique strengths of neurodivergent individuals, companies can cultivate innovation, creativity and resilience within their teams.

INSIGHT: Neurodiversity and gender

To learn more about the fundamentals of neurodiversity, I spoke to the scientist, neurodiversity and intersectionality leader and educator Dr Samantha Hiew about the underpinnings of neurodiversity, particularly in relation to gender.

Samantha told me, 'There are some differences in the way we present neurodiverse traits as males and females, but a lot of differences in individuals we need to map out off the back of our life experience and the stage of our lives.' Samantha believes 'there are generic and general differences in terms of women with ADHD appearing more inattentive, often people-pleasing, anxious or depressed, but that's just the tip of the iceberg.' Beyond this, Samantha has noted that 'there are a lot of challenges in socialization, the way we've been brought up, the rules that women have to abide by to be considered a good member of society and because of that so many women are flying under the radar because they were seen as being overly helpful, or overtly people-pleasing, trying to stay within the tribe and go unnoticed. The hyperactivity that you can see with ADHD is more internalized in girls, even from a young age, because of how parents talk to you, or how your teachers talk to you, and there are different roles given to men, girls, boys, etc. Girls are expected to be more helpful, to behave well, and it's a societal control, it's almost like a gender control.'

Growing up in Asia, she had to endure an upbringing where she was seen and not heard and she believes this experience of having parents who say 'Just be quiet, do as you're told, don't misbehave' resonates with many women across the world.

But Samantha said, 'As those girls grow up and become women, you internalize a lot of challenges, and they turn into mental health challenges. So that's how women often can have that persistent anxiety and depression, and why so many end up getting misdiagnosed even before they get to the label of ADHD or autism, or some other neurodiversity.

'Adding autism to the mix on top of all that is almost a recipe for eclectic coping strategies, and for mental health challenges it becomes something like rejection sensitivity dysphoria, where women can have increased emotional dysregulation to perceived criticisms and that can make it really hard to stay in a job.'

Samantha suggested that 'while that is one issue for women and if we are looking more at gender differences and how, for example, with ADHD as a case, we present as men and women, there is a general archetype.' She stated that 'there is a unifying archetype such as with women. They tend to double down more; they try harder and then if they don't manage to fulfil expectation they can go through meltdown or shut down rapidly. And with men they tend to take on the "class clown" persona, which feels more acceptable to them socially, but that most often leads to overwhelm, with intense masking through your life and then that overwhelm is when you can feel burnout or feel like your mental health is not in a good place. A lot of men tend not to talk about their feelings with groups of friends like women do, so they tend to dissociate and internalize these challenges.'

Research from the National Library of Medicine and the National Centre for Biotechnology Information in the USA has actually shown that men with ADHD have less ability to handle stress on their body and this leads to elevated cortisol at the perceived point of stress. And that's going to happen if the man perceives that the threat/challenge is going to happen, because your body first spikes in terms of cortisol levels because of that challenge with dealing with stress, and so a lot of men will traditionally fall back on their coping strategy to deal with pain and stress. In our culture, that often means alcohol or other vices.[20]

What Samantha attested to is that 'with women it all begins with yourself, because by the age of 12, as young girls, they have already been hurt, as they have already heard over 20,000 negative messages about themselves. And so that contributes to a distorted sense of self-esteem. In addition to this, when you layer on the gender roles in society, there are a lot of women who end up with ADHD.'

Samantha went on to state, 'Your executive functioning, your brain frontal lobe that is in charge of your day-to-day tasks, the brain control centre, is mentally three to four years delayed with ADHD compared to your peers. So, you've got children going into school and even though it doesn't change their intelligence levels, it does affect their ability to listen to instructions, to follow through, to organize themselves and to make sure they retain everything that they're meant to remember at school. And if they have those additional developmental challenges then they are going to wonder, "What is going on with me?" This becomes more confused by the way your brain works and then you actually feel misunderstood when someone says, "Why are you like this?" and you don't have the answers or "Why are you distracted?" or "Why didn't you remember to bring your science kit?" and then you go into detention, so all these things have an impact on your self-esteem because you can't trust yourself.'

Samantha believes that so many women have developed these kinds of coping strategies and had to be hyper-controlling and have really high standards for themselves because they learned that it's all or nothing. If they don't become a perfectionist in this way, then the mindset is that all hell can break loose.

Part of understanding who you are when you get diagnosed and knowing how your brain works is to figure out where your happy medium is. Otherwise, how do you learn to accept yourself and be compassionate about who you are and be kind to yourself? Because if you can't be kind to yourself, you cannot do anything outside of that to be kind to other people.

It's important that women don't forget how to be themselves, otherwise you don't know how to voice your authentic needs because you think that in order to feel good about yourself, you have to reach a certain echelon. So, what should be important to you is to root yourself to a purpose, try to exercise your authentic needs, learn to ask for things that you really need and stop people-pleasing.

As human beings, we have to learn how to be authentic without selling ourselves out. Learn how to communicate your value, learn how to self-advocate without shooting yourself in the foot. Whether it's for connection or for self-empowerment, or to find yourself, you have to be led by a purpose and attach yourself to that purpose and not to the outcome.

One of the key issues is that neurodiversity is talked about as if it represents just one type of person, rather than a plurality. In addition, many individuals will also come from a culture where they are not like 99 per cent of the people in the room. A comparison can be drawn between the experiences of those with intersectional identities and those who are neurodivergent, compounding the challenge for those who are both intersectional and neurodiverse.

I asked Samantha, based on what she knows now, if she was diagnosed again tomorrow, what would be the first three steps she would take to engage with or better understand her diagnosis. And she told me, 'To be honest, I wouldn't really do anything differently, given my time again, because I took a deep dive into everything that surrounded my diagnosis after I was given the detail.' However, Samantha did tell me that she 'would try and learn more from talking to people with lived experience rather than simply believing what the literature says'. She'd prefer to learn from what the facts are saying, because she has 'a real problem with how people talk about neurodivergence and mental health, as it is very disempowering', and for her that's why self-advocacy after you get diagnosed is the way to go. If you're telling people, whether it's your partner, or your workplace, or your friends, about your diagnosis, Samantha believes that 'needs to come from a place that is balanced, so they can understand that it's not just a deficit or a disorder. It's important that people understand you when the narrative is coming from a place of strength, the reality of your life and challenges and how you have overcome them. This should lead how you speak about your diagnosis. And speak about yourself so that people understand that your neurodiversity is only one piece of the puzzle and that you as an individual are so much more than just that. People need to understand that we're all different and talk about us as though we all bring something to the table, whether it's good or bad.'

Samantha also said that one thing she definitely wouldn't do is isolate herself, because initially she threw herself into work and then disconnected her environment and 'it came with a lot of additional challenges that weren't worth it. Sometimes it needs to be done while you are processing a lot of the trauma but in the end, it will always be far more revolutionary, if our biggest need is to be understood, to try and build bridges rather than live as an island.'

Conclusion

There's a lot to unpack here, not only in the context of Samantha's story and suggestions. From a perspective of the fundamentals, I would say that the conversation around Elon Musk's success and Asperger's syndrome serves as an opportunity to promote understanding, challenge stereotypes and foster inclusive workplaces that embrace the diverse talents of individuals, regardless of their neurological differences. However, it's pretty clear that his personal dynamic and neurodivergence has served him well because he has been able to cultivate it effectively over his many years in business.

It's clear that the ability to see opportunities where others might not, coupled with resilience and adaptability, positions neurodivergent entrepreneurs for seemingly greater success than the average neurotypical. But, moreover, entrepreneurship also offers the flexibility to create customized work environments that cater to individual needs. Neurodivergent individuals can design businesses that prioritize sensory considerations, provide flexible schedules and embrace diverse communication styles, fostering a culture of inclusivity and innovation. This is why I've run my own businesses since I was 20 years old, because I understand that value of my intellectual property and I recognize that investing in a neurodiverse mind is a little bit like pricing up artwork.

On a personal level, and having heard Samantha's experience and insights, it's also clear that embracing neurodiversity involves self-acceptance and understanding. Neurodivergent individuals may face societal expectations and pressures to conform to neurotypical norms, but if companies can help them to develop a sense of identity that embraces neurodiversity, acknowledging strengths and addressing challenges positively, then they can also massively contribute to the person's overall wellbeing.

And if you yourself suffer sometimes as I do, or Samantha does, then engaging in self-advocacy and seeking supportive communities can also provide a sense of belonging and validation. Additionally, nurturing personal interests and passions allows us neurodivergent human beings to channel our energy into areas where we can excel and find fulfilment on an emotional level.

The thing to remember here is that embracing neurodiversity is not only a matter of recognizing the inherent worth and dignity of every individual but also an acknowledgment of the diverse strengths and perspectives that neurodivergent individuals bring to the table when they're involved in running a business.

The benefits of neurodiversity extend beyond the individual to encompass the collective success of communities and organizations as a whole. By fostering cognitive diversity, promoting creativity and innovation and championing social justice, we can ensure that neurodiversity contributes to a more inclusive and resilient society. Even though challenges and misconceptions will often persist, efforts in advocacy, education, intersectionality and workplace inclusion will aid in gradually dismantling barriers and creating a more accepting environment for neurodivergent staff.

As our global society continues to evolve, embracing neurodiversity will play a pivotal role in shaping a future where every individual, regardless of their neurological makeup, can achieve success and fulfilment in every aspect of their life, and prejudice will hopefully simply fall by the wayside.

Notes

1   J Harris. The mother of neurodiversity: How Judy Singer changed the world, *The Guardian*, 5 July 2023. www.theguardian.com/world/2023/jul/05/the-mother-of-neurodiversity-how-judy-singer-changed-the-world (archived at https://perma.cc/2WU9-94W9)

2   Therapeutic Pathways. How many people have autism? Therapeutic Pathways, 2 January 2021. www.tpathways.org/faqs/how-many-people-have-autism (archived at https://perma.cc/Q93K-GDAX)

3   P Song, M Zha, Q Yang et al. The prevalence of adult attention-deficit hyperactivity disorder: A global systematic review and meta-analysis, *Journal of Global Health*, 2021, 11. www.ncbi.nlm.nih.gov/pmc/articles/PMC7916320 (archived at https://perma.cc/26Q5-4P9N)

4   Y Diena. 73 dyslexia statistics and facts: How many people have dyslexia? Ambitions, 28 July 2023. www.ambitionsaba.com/resources/dyslexia-statistics (archived at https://perma.cc/NHP5-729W)

5   Dyspraxia DCD America. What is dyspraxia/DCD?, 2019.
www.dyspraxiadcdamerica.org/what-is-dyspraxia-dcd/ (archived at https://
perma.cc/CRL7-MKBA)

6   Special Olympics. What is intellectual disability?, nd. www.specialolympics.
org/about/intellectual-disabilities/what-is-intellectual-disability (archived at
https://perma.cc/56WL-5FXV)

7   Purdue University. Largest worldwide Tourette syndrome genetics and
neuroimaging study also promises insight into related disorders, 11 May 2022.
https://www.purdue.edu/newsroom/releases/2022/Q2/largest-worldwide-
tourette-syndrome-genetics-and-neuroimaging-study-also-promises-
insight-into-related-disorders.html (archived at https://perma.cc/3VAB-ZES6)

8   S Zauderer. Key OCD Statistics: What percentage of people have OCD? Cross
River Therapy, 11 January 2023. www.crossrivertherapy.com/ocd-statistics
(archived at https://perma.cc/UF6Z-7L98)

9   Wikipedia. Epidemiology of schizophrenia, 2024. en.wikipedia.org/wiki/
Epidemiology_of_schizophrenia (archived at https://perma.cc/X9DB-9URE)

10 British Dyslexia Association. About dyscalculia, 2024. www.bdadyslexia.org.
uk/dyscalculia/how-can-i-identify-dyscalculia (archived at https://perma.cc/
A52W-EJDV)

11 M-S Ong, I Kohane, T Kai et al. Population-level evidence for an autoimmune
etiology of epilepsy, NIH, 1 May 2015. www.ncbi.nlm.nih.gov/pmc/articles/
PMC4324719/ (archived at https://perma.cc/UGD5-GB7A)

12 National Institute of Mental Health. Bipolar disorder, National Comorbidity
Survey Replication (NCS-R) (2001–03), nd. www.nimh.nih.gov/health/
statistics/bipolar-disorder (archived at https://perma.cc/DHW3-ACC4)

13 Rethink Mental Illness. Borderline personality disorder, 2024. www.rethink.org/
advice-and-information/about-mental-illness/learn-more-about-conditions/
borderline-personality-disorder-bpd/ (archived at https://perma.cc/TPG4-QXUU)

14 N Washington and J Fletcher. What to know about the relationship between
bipolar (BD) and neurodiversity, Medical News Today, 30 June 2022. www.
medicalnewstoday.com/articles/bipolar-neurodivergent (archived at https://
perma.cc/SJT3-Z6H3); M Sanches. The limits between bipolar disorder and
borderline personality disorder: A review of the evidence, NIH, 5 July 2019.
www.ncbi.nlm.nih.gov/pmc/articles/PMC6787615/ (archived at https://perma.
cc/X4K7-QUG8)

15 J Fermin. Neurodiversity in the workplace: Benefits and strategies, Medium, 6
June 2023. jeffreyfermin.medium.com/neurodiversity-in-the-workplace-benefits-
and-strategies-3baa7ea4cf19 (archived at https://perma.cc/ABY5-3CWW)

16 R Austin and G Pisano. Neurodiversity as a competitive advantage, *Harvard
Business Magazine Review*, May/June 2017. hbr.org/2017/05/neurodiversity-
as-a-competitive-advantage (archived at https://perma.cc/9VE4-NB2A)

17   A McFee. Neurodiversity: Embracing differences in education and employment, EHL Insights, 13 July 2023. hospitalityinsights.ehl.edu/neurodiversity-education-employment (archived at https://perma.cc/25DH-JGW2)

18   BBC News. Elon Musk reveals he has Asperger's on Saturday Night Live, 9 May 2021. www.bbc.co.uk/news/world-us-canada-57045770 (archived at https://perma.cc/VM94-6LA5)

19   P Shah, L Hargitai and L Livingstone. Elon Musk: How being autistic may make him think differently, The Conversation, 14 November 2022. theconversation.com/elon-musk-how-being-autistic-may-make-him-think-differently-194228 (archived at https://perma.cc/TP9S-H2HU)

20   M Corominas-Roso, G Palomar, R Ferrer et al. Cortisol response to stress in adults with attention deficit hyperactivity disorder, NIH/IJNP, 18 July 2015. www.ncbi.nlm.nih.gov/pmc/articles/PMC4576517/ (archived at https://perma.cc/A7KF-LJGT)

2

The challenges of neurodiversity vocationally

Five core issues

So, where do we begin with this issue? Ultimately, I believe there are five core aspects to the problem that each need addressing:

- societal perceptions and stigma
- workplace accommodations
- career development and advancement
- mental health and wellbeing
- lack of leadership commitment

For simplicity, lets tackle these aspects in turn.

Societal perceptions and stigma

One of the most significant obstacles that neurodivergent individuals encounter in their vocations is the pervasive societal misunderstanding around each diagnosis, and the associated stigma attached to the assumption surrounding an individual who might sit within a spectrum. These misconceptions stem from a lack of social and vocational awareness and contribute to biases that hinder the full integration of neurodivergent individuals into the workforce.

There are two core categories here:

STEREOTYPES AND PRECONCEIVED NOTIONS

Neurodivergent individuals must often contend with stereotypes that oversimplify and misrepresent their abilities. For instance, individuals on the autism spectrum may be unfairly stereotyped as socially inept or lacking in creativity, which is a complete falsehood. These sorts of stereotypes not only limit opportunities for neurodivergent human beings, but also perpetuate harmful societal biases, making it challenging for them to secure and maintain employment, and this assumptive judgement must be resolved if we are to evolve our thinking.

DISCRIMINATION AND PREJUDICE

There is still so much societal stigma surrounding neurodivergent conditions that this can lead to outright discrimination and prejudice in the workplace. Neurodivergent individuals may face challenges during the hiring process, where biases against their conditions may result in employers overlooking their qualifications and potential contributions, because at this point those people are not judged on their track record but more likely off the back of assumptive judgements surrounding a role specification and how they might perform. Additionally, discriminatory practices can manifest in unequal opportunities for career advancement and professional development, which essentially hinders the company above all, because a lack of neurodiverse hiring may be seen as easier to manage in the short term, but the longer-term gains are far greater if you're willing to put a little thought into how to cultivate an individual, or set in place some frameworks to support someone so that they may thrive in a role and feel valued as part of the collective.

Workplace accommodations

Creating a supportive work environment requires an understanding of the unique needs of those who identify as neurodivergent. While some organizations are making strides in providing accommodations, there is still a long way to go in terms of ensuring that neurodivergent individuals have the resources they need to thrive in their vocations. And, ultimately, it's not so complicated; most people misconstrue what is required and assume that we might need some sort of carer to get through the day, whereas in fact when you're neurodivergent you're generally pretty successful when autonomous and often fit into teams really well because you are more adaptive and attune to others' needs and emotions. That aside, considerations to keep in mind when supporting neurodiverse workplace wellbeing consist of:

SENSORY SENSITIVITIES
Many neurodivergent individuals experience heightened sensitivities to stimuli such as noise, light or touch. This means that the conventional workplace environment, often bustling with activity, can be overwhelming. But fear not, simple accommodations like noise-cancelling headphones, adjustable lighting or designated quiet spaces can make a substantial difference in creating a more comfortable work environment for neurodivergent individuals, and those elements are easy for any company to implement without needing big budgets.

COMMUNICATION CHALLENGES
Some individuals who are neurodivergent may face difficulties in communication, particularly in navigating social nuances and non-verbal cues. Implementing clear and explicit communication strategies, such as written instructions, visual aids and structured feedback sessions can help bridge the communication gap and enable neurodivergent individuals to understand and execute tasks effectively. And, ultimately, most decent leaders will do this with everyone in their team anyway, so implementing a little more attention in this context for those who are neurodiverse will make a huge difference in their productivity, creativity and output.

FLEXIBILITY IN WORK STRUCTURES
Traditional work structures may not cater to the diverse needs of neurodivergent individuals, so providing flexible working arrangements, including options for remote work, flexible hours and

job-sharing opportunities, allows anyone deemed as neurodivergent to tailor their work environment to better suit their strengths and challenges. Since Covid, most companies are already seeing huge demands for flexible work structures from all their staff, so this should be something companies are already considering, and for neurodiverse employees it could revolutionize their level of balance, so, again, it's a simple consideration that is easy to execute with the use of technology.

Career development and advancement

Another major issue in terms of tackling neurodiversity in business is the barriers in career development, impeding the individual's ability to advance within their chosen fields. The lack of inclusive practices and understanding can hinder professional growth and limit neurodivergent employees' access to opportunities for skill development and career progression. Some examples of this include:

LIMITED MENTORSHIP OPPORTUNITIES

Mentorship plays a crucial role in professional development, providing guidance, support and valuable insights. But the challenge comes because neurodivergent staff may face obstacles in accessing mentorship opportunities due to the prevailing misconceptions about their capabilities. Establishing mentorship programmes specifically designed to support neurodivergent individuals can help bridge this gap and foster their career development. You will better understand people's needs if you actually ask them what might help them thrive, and you'll often find that needs are far simpler to address if you are open about your willingness to offer support. In a recent neurodiversity round-table session at the Mad World Summit in London, most neurodiverse business leaders agreed that they prefer someone to ask them what they needed in order to excel, and that leadership should not fear asking questions in order to better understand the most appropriate approach to support. If we sit awkwardly and assume that neurodivergent staff will be made uncomfortable, then we miss the opportunity to innovate or to help individuals thrive.

WORKPLACE CULTURE AND ACCEPTANCE

Within any business, the overall workplace culture significantly influences the career trajectory of neurodivergent staff. A lack of awareness and acceptance within the workplace can lead to isolation and hinder collaboration. Promoting a culture of acceptance, understanding and diversity is essential in creating an environment where neurodivergent individuals feel valued and included. This also transcends just the neurodiverse, so culture is key. Understanding your values as a business should always be paramount, and in my personal experience companies who are more focused on mission as opposed to value and impact struggle to grow as rapidly as those who embrace wider cultural considerations.

UNCONSCIOUS BIAS IN HIRING AND PROMOTIONS

Unconscious bias in hiring and promotions perpetuates the challenges faced by neurodivergent individuals. Employers may unintentionally favour neurotypical candidates, overlooking the unique skills and perspectives neurodivergent individuals bring to the table. Even now, it's probably safer for those who are neurodivergent not to mention this at interview stage, because of the aforementioned stigma and bias attached, but this has to change so people are free to be themselves, and we have to cherish and cultivate those who are open because if you know yourself then you are, more often than not, someone who consistently delivers, as opposed to those who hide their true self and shy away from their individuality! Implementing training programmes to raise awareness about unconscious bias and fostering inclusive hiring and promotion practices are crucial steps toward creating a fair and equitable professional landscape and improving workplace wellbeing across the board.

Mental health and wellbeing

Based on my personal experience and some of the stories I've shared in this book so far, but also from speaking to many individuals across various businesses in many industries, I know that the challenges faced by neurodivergent human beings in their vocations can take a toll on their mental health and overarching wellbeing. Recognizing and addressing these challenges is essential for creating a workplace environment that supports the mental health of all employees across the board. Some points that I always think are prevalent to consider are:

COPING WITH WORKPLACE STRESS

Neurodivergent individuals may experience heightened stress in the workplace due to factors such as sensory overload, social anxiety or the pressure to conform to neurotypical norms. Implementing stress management programmes, promoting a supportive work culture and providing resources for coping with workplace stress are crucial components of fostering mental wellbeing among neurodivergent employees. I know that prejudice and micromanagement has hindered me in a number of roles over the years and it's so important to consider both the proactive and reactive approaches to stress management/prevention when you build out the foundations of any sustainable workplace wellbeing strategy.

BUILDING A SUPPORTIVE COMMUNITY

In addition to tackling stress head on, creating a supportive community within the workplace is vital for the mental health of neurodivergent individuals, as with any neurotypical staff. Employee resource groups focused on neurodiversity can provide a platform for sharing experiences, fostering camaraderie and advocating for policies that promote inclusivity and support. Part of my work is to help my clients to develop their own Neurodiverse Leaders Collective internally. What this means is that I work with HR/people leaders to find neurodiverse staff who want to volunteer for the greater good of their colleagues and the business in tangent. The Neurodiverse Leaders Collective serves two functions: firstly, to help businesses support their neurodiverse staff, while utilizing the raft of unique skills those staff have to offer, for the betterment of business values, drivers, culture and innovation; and secondly, to bring together neurodivergent individuals to support one another in every aspect of life through shared experience, almost like any good peer-to-peer support programme. In addition, this serves as an internal 'think tank' that could inspire a whole raft of innovations for the business that create more efficient and effective business processes, incremental revenue and far greater overarching productivity.

Lack of leadership commitment

One of the most critical factors when it comes to the success of any neurodiversity initiatives is leadership commitment. Without buy-in from top-level executives and business leaders across your organization, companies may struggle to implement meaningful changes that promote the inclusion of neurodivergent staff on a sustainable level. And there is simply no point in doing wellbeing for the sake of wellbeing. If you don't look at mental health and wellbeing from the perspective that you want to create a sustainable foundation that stands the test of time, then you're simply wasting time and money for the lip service. Staff won't therefore buy into your initiatives, and you lose every time. It's paramount that you think about the short-, medium- and long-term goals and ambitions for any strategy and have key performance indicators when it comes to the execution of the said initiatives. Without calls to action that relate to a definitive strategy your work will simply become another white paper on what's nice to have and you won't move the needle for change. So, think about what's lacking when you consider your approach to common issues such as:

FAILURE TO PRIORITIZE DIVERSITY AND INCLUSION

When leadership fails to prioritize diversity and inclusion, neurodiversity initiatives may remain on the periphery of organizational priorities. A lack of commitment can result in insufficient resources, inadequate training and a failure to create a culture that values neurodiversity as a strategic asset. And this would be a failure on the part of the business because, as I've made evident, there is so much innovation to be gained if you get this right. You will increase productivity, reduce absenteeism and encourage the cultural values that will help you thrive as a business if you focus on this issue with an objective lens. This will give you clarity and the rewards that come with it.

LIMITED ROLE MODELS

There's a big issue when it comes to the absence of neurodivergent role models in leadership positions, and this can further perpetuate the notion that neurodivergent individuals are not suited for higher-level roles. So, by proactively promoting diversity in leadership positions, including neurodivergent employees, you can challenge standardized stereotypes and demonstrate the value of diverse perspectives at all levels of the organization. This empowers not only those who are neurodivergent, but also those who see themselves as diverse in any capacity.

If you grow up never truly understanding who you are then the road ahead may seem bleak. I spent my formative years in a damaging and volatile environment, so my default setting as a young boy was to compartmentalize, to disengage mentally and try to find solace in whatever I could. Whether that be a great work of fiction, like the writings of Brian Jacques and his tales of Redwall, or a movie that lost me to the possibility that anything was achievable, I'd often try to disappear in the narrative, so I didn't have to suffer my own reality.

There was no diagnosis for me at that time. My twin brother had died when we were young, so while I didn't fully understand that back then, I always felt like I was missing a part of me and I suppose in many ways I just didn't know where that empty space came from.

This means that it took me a long time, throughout my education and moving into the world of work later, to fully establish who I was or what I truly wanted or needed from a vocation. I had some dreams and some life goals, as many of us do growing up, but there was not a lot of direction around anything outside that, so not only was I growing up trying to understand who I was, I was also dealing with the inevitable challenges when leaving home and trying to define what I wanted to do with my life or what sort of vocation might best support my neurodiversity – or at least what I knew at the time was a diverse mindset and perception of the world around me. And without guidance toward a vocation, I believe it's almost impossible for a neurodivergent individual to find a path that isn't fraught with extremities and challenges.

The challenges neurodiverse employees face

As our understanding of neurodiversity grows, it becomes crucial to address the challenges faced by neurodivergent individuals as they evolve through education and into the workplace. Employment is such a fundamental aspect of adult life, providing not only financial independence but also a sense of purpose and social inclusion. However, the traditional workplace often poses unique obstacles for neurodivergent individuals. And part of my reason behind writing this book is to explore the challenges we encounter in our vocations, shedding light on societal perceptions, workplace accommodations and the importance of fostering an inclusive environment. As I touched on in the previous chapter, I also think it's important to look more deeply at the benefits of hiring someone who is neurodivergent, because while diversity and inclusion efforts have gained some momentum in recent years, the workplace still presents hurdles for neurodivergent individuals seeking to build meaningful and sustainable careers.

My conclusion, when it comes to fostering diversity, is that neurodivergent individuals face a myriad of challenges in their vocations, ranging from these societal perceptions and workplace accommodations, through to their career development and mental health, and addressing these challenges requires a comprehensive and concerted effort from both employers and society at large.

If you as a company or senior leader focus on dispelling stereotypes, implementing tailored accommodations, fostering inclusive workplace cultures and prioritizing mental health, then organizations can create environments where neurodivergent individuals not only survive but thrive in their professional pursuits.

As we move forward, it is imperative that we dismantle barriers, challenge biases and work towards a future where neurodivergent individuals are valued, included and given equal opportunities to contribute their unique talents to the professional landscape.

It is so evident, based on all that I've seen over two decades in business, that the untapped potential of neurodiverse staff remains a missed opportunity for many companies, rooted in misconceptions, inadequate awareness and the absence of inclusive practices. Furthermore, to fully realize the benefits of neurodiversity, organizations must actively challenge stereotypes, invest in comprehensive training and awareness programmes, implement inclusive hiring practices and secure leadership commitment to prioritize diversity and inclusion.

It is only through fostering a workplace culture that values and leverages neurodiversity that companies will not only enhance their ability to attract and retain diverse talent, but also promote innovation, creativity and overall organizational success. As we move forward, it is imperative that companies recognize the richness that neurodivergent individuals bring to the professional landscape and take proactive steps to build workplaces that celebrate diversity in all its forms.

INSIGHT: Thriving and getting the right support at work

In researching the biggest challenges facing someone with neurodiversity when it comes to vocation, I met a really inspiring individual on a journey to find his fit and define a career that made him feel valued for the dynamism and creativity that he holds and that we should all hope to achieve.

Jonathan Wakefield is a young man who has seen more working environments than the average individual because of consistently poor leadership approaches to cultivating his unique needs, as someone who is diagnosed as having ADHD and identifies as autistic, for which he is undergoing a ridiculously lengthy process of diagnosis. The combination of autism and ADHD is ever-more prevalent, but possibly the most challenging aspect is being taken seriously or being looked after during process of diagnosis by employers as you develop your career, or even just struggle to make ends meet.

In interviewing Jonathan about his work experience throughout his life, it was evident that most of his managers over the years had simply failed to recognize that there were steps they could take to get the best out of him and his work ethic. So, I wanted to delve into some of that. Most of us can probably relate to having a few random jobs during our career, but I thought the scale and variety that Jonathan had endured was really interesting. He has ultimately had a raft of random jobs in his life that didn't fit, either because he just didn't feel valued, or his needs were not well managed, so I asked him to detail a few for context.

Jonathan admitted that he'd certainly been through the mill a bit over the years but had gained so much experience in so many areas that he feels all his experience has led to the man he is today and to understanding what he truly needs from his peers and leaders. Jonathan has worked as a FedEx package handler, a personal assistant to a vicar, a families worker for a charity, a bar-back and a cocktail waiter. He's worked in cybersecurity and as a recruiter, and now has finally found his fit as a travel consultant. Having worked all over the world in such a wide range of industries, Jonathan states with fervour that, so far, he feels that his role as a travel consultant has 'best fit who he is', his internal dynamic and his ability to manage a positive work–life balance. Rather unusually, Jonathan grew up in an international family that was full of pilots, and so throughout his formative years and beyond he 'had the opportunity to travel a lot more than the average individual'. There was actually even a point in his life where he wanted to become a commercial pilot, but because of his ADHD he wasn't allowed to pursue this as a career, even though some might say that the hyper awareness that comes with ADHD, might actually aid individuals who are performing the sort of task where they might need to be highly adaptive and engaged in multiple things all at once. None the less, as much as that was a tough pill to swallow, Jonathan feels that his 'travel experience really lends itself to his role as a travel consultant' and he can finally invest in developing his career in an industry he's had a lifelong passion for.

With Jonathan trying over the years to find a vocation that fit his existential needs, I was also interested to find out whether there was a common theme among managers that led to him to jump from job to job for so many years and what interested me greatly was that he did sense a broadly common theme.

Jonathan told me, 'I consistently felt internally that my managers, regardless of the type of job, or the tasks required within that role, would never truly trust me to get the job done.' Still further, he felt that 'they also never expected me to do it well. It was quite common and very obvious to me on numerous occasions that they were even surprised when I actually had success or executed tasks efficiently or effectively, and this was quite undermining. In addition, because of this stigma and preconception, I always found myself being constantly micro-managed and could never fully utilize my skills, personality or creativity to the fullest, and I believe that this played a big part in holding me back greatly.'

It's actually tragic to hear that Jonathan had this experience in so many roles, and I know that there will be people out there making the obvious assumptions that maybe he was over-thinking his experience, or that if you experience the same thing again and again it might be because of personal factors, but to be honest, I've had the same issue in my career, as have many of my peers, and the sad fact is that as soon as you tell people in a work context about your diagnosis, there's a seed of doubt cast upon you. People may not want to accept it, but there's a layer of inbuilt prejudice that overshadows the neurodivergent in business and this is why we fear being honest and open about our diagnoses. It's easier just to get on with the job and keep a low profile than it is to be open and expect our true selves to be honoured as they should be.

As someone who identifies as autistic, as Jonathan is still under diagnosis and living with ADHD on top of that, I wondered what it was that Jonathan felt he needed most in a vocation to make him feel safe and effective in his role. Jonathan mentioned during our discussion that this was something that he'd wondered about many times over the years.

He surmised, 'There's always a challenge when you think about what you want to do career-wise and what your needs are, because you never think that a company will care enough to invest in your needs, but actually something that I never considered, yet have in my life now, is a professional coach.' Jonathan said that he's 'found that having the ability to see and speak to a trained professional and being given the flexibility to do this by my company, has helped me feel much safer internally as a human being and it's really impacted on how much more effective I am in my work day-to-day. I simply spend an hour with an ADHD coach every two weeks and she has been wonderful in respect of helping me tackle personal and professional challenges at work. And I personally think for most businesses this is something that could be an easy and affordable gateway to improving their employees' lives if they register as neurodivergent.'

What Jonathan mentions here is a really important point. As someone who runs individual and group coaching for my clients, I find that when you help someone on a base level to tap into who they are as a human being, not just necessarily in their career capacity, but bridging the gap between their work and home life, they are far more fulfilled off the back of it, and most often become more present and far more productive. There are always training budgets set aside for companies to do team building, or workshops for various things that relate to the role itself, but it's a little rarer to find companies who want to help their people on a wider level. Part of the issue with absenteeism and low productivity often comes down to what's going on outside the office or working environment, so with companies often being reticent about telling their employees how to live, a good coaching programme to work with people to tackle what's holding them back in life on a general level can be really impactful. You will find that investing in your people in this way will not only gain wider engagement in who you are as a business or brand, but it will make your employees more enthusiastic and confident when they take to their desks to execute their role. So, what's to lose? It costs 10 times more money to find a new Jonathan, than it does to invest a little bit of money in someone who can help him be effective at work.

I talked with Jonathan on a number of occasions about his raft of poor experience over the years in his career, so I thought it might be poignant to acknowledge what the most negative experience he'd had with a leader/manager was, which he feels was due to their not understanding Jonathan's neurodivergent needs as an individual.

Rather ironically, Jonathan suggested, 'My worst experience was actually while working for a recruitment agency where I had a line manager who had another team member with ADHD and tried with gusto to manage me and my ADHD colleague in the same way. That being said, I don't think many people realize that there are multiple facets to ADHD and that you are generally either "hyperactive" or "inattentive". The problem in this scenario was that the other ADHD team member was hyperactive, and I was classified as ADHD inattentive. So, in this instance, my manager either couldn't (or chose not to) understand the difference between the two differing diagnoses, and this led to oppressive micro-management, miscommunication and ultimately an inevitable breakdown in our working relationship.' So, in the end, Jonathan decided to find a role where he might be better understood and managed in a way that felt safe and more engaging.

Jonathan now has a range of productive habits that he's employed personally to make him more effective in business and stabilize his day-to-day work–life balance, so I thought I'd also look at what his regime is, as it may inspires others to follow suit.

Firstly, Jonathan has a routine that sets him up for the day and builds on putting him in the right headspace every morning. It's regular and he keeps rigidly to the same routine each workday, as it helps to provide him with consistency and the right momentum. 'I don't like to use my phone for the first part of the day, and I've also removed everything that is work-related from my phone to enable myself to properly shut off once I'm outside work or the working environment. But, essentially, when my alarm goes off I say, "Good morning, Alexa" and the phone will turn my bedroom light on and start playing things like the morning news, which may seem mundane and a bit dismal with some of the news we've been having in recent months, but I find it is a good way to slowly start to wake up my brain and stimulate my senses. After some time, Alexa will play the weather to let me know what the world is looking like outside, so if the weather is good then I'm feeling immediately positive and if the weather is looking bleak then at least I wake up with the mindset that I need to wear a jacket or have an umbrella to hand, and this helps me to be mentally ready to face whatever might befall me.'

After the weather report, Jonathan heads to the bathroom to begin his shower and teeth brushing routine, though he mentioned 'the fewer specifics surrounding that, the better, I guess. And when I leave the bathroom, I always leave the light on, as a reminder that I need to take my medication, while I head off to get dressed for the day. After that I hit the kitchen to get my lunch together, grab my water, pack my bag and then return to the bathroom to take my medication, before instructing Alexa to turn off all the lights, and I leave the apartment for work.'

Beyond this, Jonathan has also built healthy habits such as 'getting up from my desk for 10 minutes every hour, on the hour, and just going for a walk, leaving the office to get some fresh air. I also make sure I have some kind of sugar/sweet treat ready for the afternoon to avoid any medication crash once my meds start to wear off. This keeps me focused and grounded and ensures that I don't hit a slump during the last part of the working day.'

There is an important point there on the medication front, as it's something that many individuals will have to tackle. When I was first diagnosed as being on the bipolar spectrum and was suffering from extreme bouts of depression and suicidal ideation, I was given medication which actually really worked for me until around 3pm in the afternoon. Following that, I couldn't string a sentence together, which in itself is a nightmare, especially when you're in a sales role, as I was at the time, because it's not conducive to closing a deal or making money. However, without the right support and guidance I didn't know how to manage my medication or those lapses in cognitive ability, and so I threw the medication in the bin and set about learning how to remap my mind for a more sustainable effort at evolving my vocational desires. But that's a challenge in itself. Something that companies should most certainly explore with neurodivergent staff who need to take medication is not shying away from seeking to understand how it affects them and whether there is anything that the company can provide to support this, whether that is professional advice from a clinician as to how best to manage medication, or whether it's as simple as having afternoon fruits, or sweet treats readily available for anyone who might regularly need a lift. Both initiatives are easy and cost effective to implement so it seems like a simple addition to any wider wellbeing provisions in my eyes. There's no 'quick fix' but let's think outside the box… why does your approach to your people's wellbeing have to fit a standard? If a myriad of little things makes the difference, then what's stopping you trying a variety of initiatives?

With all of the above in mind, based on how Jonathan feels he was treated and all the self-preservative prep he has built into play, I thought it would also be interesting to know, from his experience vocationally to date, what he feels employers should focus on first when tackling the subject of neurodiversity to improve on workplace culture.

The biggest thing that Jonathan suggested here was that 'every employer should be tackling this "one-size-fits-all" attitude and approach to wellbeing that so many businesses have. This could be considered more in the context of training, onboarding new staff, the hiring process and policies, or even things like company key performance indicators (KPIs) etc. The subject of neurodiversity is a difficult one to tackle, because many employers don't fully understand the needs of their neurotypical staff, let alone those who might require special conditions to be most effective. And, frankly, so many individuals involved in the people processes won't even truly know themselves or who they are, so how can employers expect them to have a handle on the unique needs of a diverse contingent of staff?' Jonathan's recommendation would be to 'bring in a specialist, someone who can properly educate HR and people leaders as to what neurodiversity, ADHD, autism spectrum disorder and the wider spectrum actually consists of and means to both the individuals who face it and the businesses they work in.' Jonathan also stated avidly, 'Companies *must* humanize it! It's never good to do it on a video and forget about teams, or pre-recorded training or commentary; you should be bringing in a human being, or a string of human beings, to build out your peoples understanding of neurodiversity on a deeper level, help them to see the assets and not just think of it as another HR hindrance. This mindset will see employers having a better handle on the needs of their neurodivergent employees and will create a far more sustainable foundation for the business moving forward when it comes to overarching wellbeing and culture.'

One size does not fit all

I think the elements that Jonathan mentioned at the end of our interview were really important. I saw that, with the introduction of wellbeing apps and employee assistant programmes over the last several years, for the most part staff are not engaged when the context from their business is to carpet-bomb wellbeing and hope that something sticks. As businesses try harder to define what approach might cater for their 'one-size-fits-all' mentality, as Jonathan mentioned, they draw further away from understanding what it truly is to be a human being and so they lose touch with the needs of their people. Later in this book I'm going to be covering some initiatives that focus on how to better develop workplace wellbeing, with suggested individuals and companies that I feel are doing more valuable and sustainable work for their clients, so I won't go into too much depth on this aspect now. However, what I will say is that companies that fail to understand the importance of more peer-to-peer support and more human engagement/interaction and are more objective in their way of thinking about how to do wellbeing more effectively will also fail to inspire those individuals across their business who want to feel seen and heard when it comes to their individualistic and collective needs. Those companies will join the dinosaurs over time, because unless you have set values and you are proactive in executing on those values, your business simply won't stand the test of time.

INSIGHT: Carving your own path

On my journey delving into some of these issues I wondered what life might look like for those who just didn't feel they could find a fit in the average office or company roles that are more prevalent once you leave school, college or university and breach the world of work for the first time. And, along the way, I decided that I wanted to interview someone who had turned his life around by shunning the traditional course of action when it came to vocation and carved his own path.

J Grange, a successful neurodiversity champion and public speaker, who has built a budding music career and even spoken at the United Nations, told me, 'I never had much hope for myself until I found music' and his early stage experiences are very similar to what I faced when I was at school based on common misconceptions and lack of engagement in understanding who we are as individuals, as opposed to trying to whitewash a collective with an overarching approach to evolving us educationally.

Instead of giving up on himself, J chose to 'define his future, face some hard truths and forge a career that made me feel whole'. But I wanted to find out what his expectations were when he left school to enter the world of work, and it came to finding a job for the long term.

J said, 'To be honest, I was excluded permanently from two separate schools because I was disengaged and disruptive in terms of my energy. In the end I was sent to a pupil referral unit, but ended up barely achieving any GCSE qualifications and I certainly didn't fancy going to university, so I ended up without a degree either. At one stage I wasn't even in education or any kind of employment at all and I ended up on universal credit, which is like a government funding scheme to help those who can't get work or afford to buy food or rent somewhere to live. So my personal expectation was that I wouldn't be able to find a job and that nobody would ever want to employ me because of my background, or because I hadn't followed the traditional "societal norms" when it came to my early-stage education.'

Now, I understood from our conversation that J wasn't confident he would be able to get a more traditional job, but I wanted to better understand what led to him feeling that he'd not necessarily engage with the average working environment and prompted him to try to forge a career in the music industry.

He told me, 'From the experience that I was having in trying to find a career path that suited me, I found that the average working environment just wasn't inclusive enough of those people like me who are neurodivergent. A lot of job applications and hiring processes aren't neurodiversity friendly, so I definitely struggled with that aspect, and workplaces need to do a lot more to be neuro-inclusive when attracting and retaining talent. I've never been the type of person to want that 9-to-5 kind of job throughout a working week. I'd also always personally wanted to be self-employed and liked the idea of being my own boss.' And, as I know only too well, a 9-to-5 job isn't for many neurodivergent people, and most will thrive more with the autonomy that comes with running their own show.

What J mentions here is prevalent and something I mentioned when I spoke about Elon Musk in my previous chapter, but while running your own business gives you autonomy there's also a lot of anxiety that comes with that. On a personal level, I never wanted to run my own business, necessarily – I simply wanted to work for someone who would look after me, cherish my assets as a human being, point me in a direction and let me fly in my own way. I just never really found that, so I decided to set up my own business. It's still something I long for today – I'd much rather someone just bought my business, took away all the administrative anxiety and let me have some autonomy to innovate, bring in business and execute the things I enjoy doing, but when you work alone you don't always have the time to explore this sort of thing and you also risk relationships that become constricting and won't allow you the ability to flourish.

That aside, if more companies thought about their neurodivergent staff as innovators, then they could better engage them to stay with the company, evolve what that company stands for and breed the feeling of safety that individuals like J and I crave when it comes to being able to exercise our creativity and autonomy. The results of this could be and are infinitely valuable to any organization, regardless of the size.

But, throughout this conversation, I constantly wondered about his period before finding music and what J felt was the most common misconception about him that led to people holding him back.

What he analysed along the way was that 'most people just thought that I was lazy, naughty and unintelligent, and that I wouldn't amount to anything, so they rarely invested any time in me. People generally couldn't see my true potential, they just didn't believe in me and only focused on my weaknesses and never my strengths. I got told constantly that I was a failure, and this led to limiting self-belief in my early years. I was told I'd end up in prison, like many people with ADHD do, and I had so many discriminatory comments made about me it was tough to believe in myself at times.'

So, this led me to ask how J felt his ADHD has made him more effective when creating music. He said, 'My biggest strength is that my ADHD allows me to think unconventionally and from a different perspective, which in turn makes me more adaptable to things and more effective when I'm working. I also use the endless amounts of creativity in my mind and put everything I can into words on paper that form the lyrics for my songs. It also makes me think more deeply and write in a way that most neurotypical people wouldn't be able to do. The thing that inspires me is that the creative industries are full of neurodivergent talent, so there's just not so much prejudice, and around 33 per cent of CEOs and entrepreneurs are neurodiverse, too, so I just have this greater sense that I belong.'

But what I wanted to know after listening to some of his tunes was why J thinks that so many people resonate with his personal approach to harnessing his neurodivergence through his music, public speaking and beyond, because there's got to be a theme here.

What J explained was that he believes his personal approach to harnessing his neurodivergence resonates with people 'because it's real and authentic and also because I primarily focus on my strengths and not the weaknesses that challenge me. I see my ADHD as an enhanced ability and not the disability that so many still consider it to be. I see more of what my community and I *can* do, as opposed to what we *can't* do, and that's a strong mindset to have. Rather than letting my past hold me back, I use my lived experience and show people my vulnerability in talking about the challenges that I've overcome to try to inspire change. I also make sure, where I can, that I educate those around me, so I often speak at schools and big corporations about neuro-inclusion, as well as how to be allies to individuals like me, because one in five will face ADHD daily. In doing this I help people understand how to be more inclusive as a society.'

It's clear that everything J does comes from a place filled with passion. But, more purposefully, he is keen to educate. I asked him what sort of advice he gives to other young people with ADHD who are struggling with education and worrying about how they might earn a living. J said, 'Most importantly, I tell them that you have to embrace your neurodivergence. It is a gift and most definitely, in my eyes, a competitive advantage if you cultivate it. Ignore those negative stereotypes and the myths that so many people automatically absorb from the society around them. I mention it's an ability and not a disability. It's important for young people to hear that because if you call something a "disorder" then it suggests a negative narrative. Your education doesn't define who you are or who you choose to become. You must find your own path, your own route through life and your own potential. Put trust in the timing of opportunities but create your own, too, and everything in time will fall into place for you.'

I think one of the most important points J made in response to that final question was that your education doesn't define who you are, or who you choose to become. I haven't been in education for two decades now. When I started in business it was widely considered that if you didn't have a degree of some kind, no matter how superfluous, then you would struggle to get a job because you couldn't prove any level of stickability. However, I have no serious qualifications outside a diploma of higher education in drama and theatre studies, and I learned how to do business by trying things and adapting and learning. I don't say this for the sake of my own ego, but one of the companies I'm involved in currently has the potential to sell for in excess of £150 million, so I guess that J is totally right, especially if his story or mine are anything to go by. You can most definitely become successful by traditional standards by treading a completely untraditional path, if you simply believe in who you are as an individual and what you have to offer the world, even if nobody else chooses to believe in you.

A 2020 article in *Rolling Stone* magazine suggested that 'The Florence and the Machine star [Florence Welch] was diagnosed with both dyslexia and dyscalculia in her youth, two sets of "learning difficulties", as she often heard them described, inaccurately, during her school years. She describes this in the foreword to *Creative Differences*, a new handbook on neurodiversity published in 2020 by Universal and aimed at employers in the creative industries. Welch says that in her first paid job, as a barmaid, she felt a "sting of shame" when her manager exposed her inability to count change. Subsequently, she devised her own ingenious remedy for this 'shortcoming', and she actually taught herself to recognize 'the shape of each coin in her hand and apply a geometric value to it. In the end, she says, she became a pretty good barmaid.' But should we have to educate ourselves? Of course, it makes us more adaptable, but surely there should be more support and education, regardless of the role or the industry.[1]

During my early primary school years my sisters were silent – they were seen and not heard – while I chose the path of the clown, the mimic, the unassailable energy that would try to light up the room for all those around me, in the vain hope that they wouldn't see the pain I was suffering deep within.

I was deemed 'the naughty boy' or 'the disruptor'. I was bullied by teachers and held back during developmental classes because they couldn't understand where to engage me and where to let me thrive off my own steam.

I remember during early English language lessons there was a process called 'look–cover–write–check'. There was a box of cards at the front of the classroom that were colour-coded, starting with colours like yellow, orange and red, and moving up in complexity into colours like green, purple, brown and black, almost like a martial arts belt system. The concept was that you had to select a card (each had around seven words on) and you would look at the words, cover the card, then write the words, subsequently uncovering the card to check if you'd nailed the spelling or not. But you were only allowed to advance to a more complex colour set when the teacher allowed you to.

I recall a teacher, one of my earliest bullies. This teacher saw me advancing through this process rapidly, ahead of most of the class. Of course, it was systematic, so I was thriving. This teacher was my class tutor, however, and perhaps she had to put up with too much of my high energy on a daily basis, so for some reason when I got to the purple card stack, somewhere in the middle level, I was halted. I would consistently memorize and write down every card in turn. I must have learned all those words off by heart before long, but every time I approached her desk with a full house of correct answers, I'd be told to repeat the process, never allowing me to get to the next level. I seemed to spend my days and weeks in this purple zone. I saw people around me catching up and starting to move beyond my level, and I was trapped in a sort of language-based *Groundhog Day*, repeating the same task over and over, and growing continually frustrated at my teacher's reticence to let me thrive when I was clearly executing what was required. I see the scenario so vividly in my mind. I remember the classroom configuration even now if I close my eyes and I have no idea why I was penalized, even to this day. But it hurt!

Further down the line, a second bully arrived on the scene: the deputy head teacher. One day, the entire year were ushered into a huge room and told to sit down cross-legged, a huge force of 10-year-old faces staring at the front, wondering what the point was, when we should be outside running around. Slowly Mr D ran through a list of names. There were maybe 10–15 children on that list, of which I was one, and we were made to go and stand up in front of the whole room full of our peers. Like a miniature parade facing an army.

The student contingent was told that those who had been singled out had each done something naughty in the last week or two and we were being chastised in this way because we needed to see the error of our ways. The students were told that they could raise their hand and suggest someone who they felt should be redeemed and allowed to try to be better, like a process of absolving us of our sins. So, one by one, a child would raise their hand and say the name of one of the sullied, and the Mr D would ask the child who'd raised their hand if they thought that person should get another chance to be good. And the child would say yes and the teacher would then allow that child to join the mass of students, thus removing themselves from their position of embarrassment. This process continued until I was the last child standing on my own, alone in front of the horde.

I remember thinking, 'Ok, my turn, one of my mates will stick up for me and I'm good to go', and sure enough, a friend of mine, Victoria, also a twin, raised her hand and said my name and she was cordially asked by the teacher if I should get another chance to be good. She responded 'yes', as all those before her who'd helped my naughty peers rejoin the wider contingent of kids. But when she said yes, Mr D responded differently to anyone else he'd allowed back into the fold previously and he said, 'Now, why don't you think that's a good idea?'

Victoria said nothing – what 10-year-old can comprehend how to answer a question like that? If the process had changed only at the end for me, then why was I any different? Why should I not be allowed to rejoin my friends, as all the other children had beforehand? The silence weighed heavy. Everyone stared at me, no one spoke. It seemed like an eternity, my heart sitting heavy in my chest as I struggled to understand why I was so bad, and what was wrong with me. After some time the teacher looked at his watch and dismissed everyone and all the children awkwardly stood up and we were ushered out.

Needless to say, I went home and cried. I told my mum and dad everything. I was fearful that they would blame me as the teachers had, but their response surprised me. They immediately removed me from that school and assured me that I wouldn't ever have to go back there. This moment probably healed me more than I realized at the time. I think if they'd thrown it in my face or chastised me at that point then I would have crumbled, but for all the challenges at home, all the volatility, they were united in that decision at that moment, and I felt safe.

The reason I mention this story is because everything in life starts with our education, the opportunity to find out who we are. As much as I consider the education system to be more about teaching a bunch of kids how to pass exams, dictated by a prescribed textbook, as opposed to developing any level of nuance surrounding how to be a worthy or evolved human being, I feel that there should be room to thrive in your educational environment and expand your mind. If given the opportunity, you're more likely to find out who you are early on, what values you hold dear and thus get some gauge for what you want to do with the rest of your life.

My great aunt had unfortunately passed away at about this time, and with my family being relatively poor she'd left my younger sister and I a bit of money in her will, which meant that my parents had some options when they took the decision to extract me from this destructive environment. They selected a private secondary school that I attended for two years. Class sizes were much smaller – about 15 children in a class – and there was one-to-one care and attention from teachers. Half the children already had French language locked down for their skiing holidays, while I still didn't really understand the concept that there were other languages, as my previous school didn't have a whiff of that type of education. There were hot school dinners every day, we had to wear blazers, carry briefcases and use fountain pens. There was a school badge, a school song (that I still remember to this day), and there were houses just like in *Harry Potter*. And, while Potter wasn't even a thought in J K Rowling's mind at this point, it was to all intents and purposes what Hogwarts must have felt like for that scruffy boy who lived under the stairs previously. It was a dream to me.

The teachers immediately saw my energy and dynamism. It truly was the happiest time I remember in my entire life. Nothing before or since has ever felt as good as that place. And, ultimately, I attribute my ability to speak in front of hundreds or thousands of people today, or to write an insightful blog, poem or piece of text that may help someone feel less alone, to the teaching I gained from that school and those few teachers who cared enough to deliver what I needed. That was truly the first opportunity in my life, still undiagnosed, to harness my neurodivergent traits and put them to use in a productive and safe environment, for the greater good of my psyche. I believe to this day that they saved me. Because they gave me the ability to take the darkness I felt internally and express myself using it – to pour anger and hate and fear and volatility onto paper and heal myself through this exploration. I will never forget them for that.

Why companies should actively hire
neurodiverse individuals

What is apparent from my findings is that, in the evolving landscape of the modern workplace, embracing neurodiversity has emerged as a crucial component in fostering innovation, creativity and overall organizational success. Neurodiverse individuals, encompassing conditions such as autism, ADHD and dyslexia, among others, bring a unique set of skills, perspectives and talents that can greatly enrich your workforce. So, I want to further highlight what should be considered the most compelling reasons why companies should actively consider hiring neurodiverse individuals.

- **Diverse perspectives and problem-solving skills:** As these interviews highlight, neurodivergent individuals often possess a distinct way of thinking and problem-solving. Their brains are wired differently, enabling them to approach challenges from unconventional angles. This diversity of thought can be a valuable asset for problem-solving, encouraging innovative solutions and fostering a culture of creativity within any organization.[2]

- **Attention to detail and precision:** Many neurodivergent individuals exhibit a high degree of attention to detail and precision in their work. This meticulousness can be particularly advantageous in roles that require accuracy, thoroughness and a keen eye for detail. From data analysis to quality control, neurodivergent individuals can excel in tasks that demand precision and most actually gain great satisfaction from executing work-based tasks in this meticulous way.[3]

- **Exceptional memory and pattern recognition:** Some neurodivergent conditions, such as autism, are associated with exceptional memory and pattern recognition abilities. This can be beneficial in roles that involve data analysis, programming or any task that requires the identification of patterns and trends. Harnessing these cognitive strengths can lead to improved efficiency and effectiveness in various job functions and can dramatically improve your business and operations across the board.

- **Dedication and loyalty:** Neurodivergent individuals often exhibit a strong sense of dedication and loyalty to their work, especially if they are made to feel safe and valued by their employer. When they find roles that align with their interests, strengths and core values, they tend to be committed and passionate employees for the long term. So, companies that embrace neurodiversity and provide a supportive environment often experience increased employee retention and satisfaction, with very minimal absenteeism.

- **Innovation and creativity:** The neurodivergent mind is often characterized by a unique approach to creativity. Companies that prioritize neurodiversity can tap into a wide range of innovative ideas and solutions consistently. By fostering an open and inclusive culture that values diverse and unique perspectives, organizations can then begin to unlock the full creative potential of their wider workforce, driving continuous innovation that not only moves the bottom line but also sets their business apart to gain an industry advantage over their competitors.

- **Adaptability and resilience:** Because of the challenging misconceptions and difficult early-stage path, like we've seen from Jonathan and J, neurodivergent individuals frequently demonstrate resilience and adaptability in the face of challenges. Why wouldn't we? We've had to overcome hardships, prejudice and misconceptions since the first day off the school bus because of the different way we operate. Overcoming societal and workplace barriers, they develop coping mechanisms and problem-solving skills that make them highly adaptable. In an ever-changing business landscape, having employees who can navigate change with resilience is a valuable asset and very often you find that neurotypicals struggle more than someone with a neurodiversity when it comes to resilience because they haven't been forced, as we have, to look so introspectively at who they are.[4]

- **Enhanced team dynamics:** The inclusion of neurodiverse individuals contributes to more dynamic and well-rounded teams. Neurodivergent employees bring a variety of strengths that complement those of their neurotypical colleagues, resulting in a collaborative and synergistic work environment. This diversity fosters a culture of mutual respect and shared learning, and it's rare that you find any ego attached when working with someone who is neurodivergent because it is common to have that stripped away before the point where we enter the world of work.

- **Positive impact on corporate culture:** A commitment to neurodiversity sends a powerful message about an organization's values and commitment to inclusivity as a whole. Embracing neurodiversity fosters a positive corporate culture that values diversity in all its forms. This, in turn, attracts a wider pool of talented individuals who appreciate and seek out workplaces that prioritize inclusivity on a foundational level. Which means that your diversity, equity and inclusion initiatives are paramount when it comes to getting the best employees for the roles you have to offer.

Conclusion

Hiring neurodiverse individuals is not just a moral imperative but a strategic advantage for companies seeking to thrive in a competitive and rapidly changing world. By recognizing and valuing the unique strengths neurodivergent individuals bring to the workforce, companies can build more innovative, adaptable and inclusive organizations. Embracing neurodiversity is not only a win for individual employees, but a win for the entire organization, unlocking untapped potential and contributing to long-term success.

So, why wouldn't you invest in that?

Notes

1 T Ingham. Are music companies hiring enough people who think differently? *Rolling Stone*, 23 January 2020. www.rollingstone.com/music/music-features/music-industry-neurodiversity-941115/ (archived at https://perma.cc/ZR4M-BZN2)

2 S Duggan. The power of thinking differently: Neurodiversity and problem solving, NALA, April 2023. nala.org/neurodiversity-and-problem-solving/ (archived at https://perma.cc/99JF-RGYL)

3 N Bowles. 30 strengths of neurodiversity: Part 1, IAM, 8 February 2024. i-am-autism.org.uk/30-strengths-of-neurodiversity-part-1 (archived at https:// perma.cc/6DQN-BSA6)

4 C Londero. Autistic children don't need to work on resilience; Neurotypical people may need to work on empathy, The Art of Autism, 10 October 2022. the-art-of-autism.com/autistic-children-dont-need-to-work-on-resilience-neurotypical-people-may-need-to-work-on-empathy/ (archived at https://perma. cc/VN8Q-25DC)

3

Dispelling the neurodiversity myths

Neurodiversity challenges traditional perspectives on neurological differences, emphasizing the inherent value of diverse cognitive styles and abilities. However, despite growing awareness, numerous myths persist surrounding neurodiversity. These myths often contribute to misunderstanding, stigma and barriers for neurodivergent individuals. In this chapter, I will explore and debunk some of the most prevalent myths, offering a more accurate and nuanced understanding of neurodiversity and its impact on individuals and society.

10 myths about neurodiversity

Most companies talk about inclusive hiring, and they may even actively interview neurodivergent, intersectional or diverse candidates, but there remains an underlying prejudice that means we are not evolving as a human race on a fundamental level when it comes to vocation, because we are failing to see that it takes a more human level of intervention to really get results in the world of workplace wellbeing. So, I thought it would be interesting to throw my top 10 myths into the mix for your consideration, because I believe that in the doing, perhaps the ripple effect of this book might shake a few trees and change a few lives or business processes along the way.

Myth 1: Neurodiversity is a new trend

One of the most common misconceptions surrounding neurodiversity is that it is a recent phenomenon or a passing trend, but that's simply not the case. In reality, the concept has roots dating back to the late 1990s when Australian sociologist Judy Singer coined the term. However, the principles of neurodiversity are not an innovative or novel discovery; ultimately, they represent a paradigm shift by challenging the medical model's pathologization of neurological differences.[1]

The neurodiversity movement essentially advocates for acknowledging and celebrating the natural variations in neurological development present in the human population. It emphasizes the idea that conditions like autism, ADHD, dyslexia and others are not defects but rather valid expressions of neurodiversity, and that different ways of thinking and operating as human beings can in fact be an asset to individuals and the people around them, as well as the organizations they work for. Understanding neurodiversity as a fundamental aspect of human variation is not a fleeting trend but a paradigm that continues to gain recognition and acceptance, in the main, because as a culture we should be celebrating all variations of diversity, as with other prevalent movements covering issues such as race and gender equality, within both society as a whole and the working environment.

Myth 2: Neurodiversity ignores the challenges faced by neurodivergent individuals

Another misconception about the neurodiversity movement is that it downplays the challenges faced by neurodivergent individuals. But, in reality, the whole concept of breaking down the stigma around neurodiversity is about advocating for recognition of the unique difficulties associated with conditions like autism, ADHD and others. The neurodiversity movement itself has ultimately focused from the very beginning on shifting the narrative from a deficit-based model to one that acknowledges both challenges and strengths, so that the neurotypical can better understand and empathize with our challenges, but also seek to become allies and to support and champion why those who think or act in a different or sometimes seemingly unusual way can also be beautiful and valuable human beings in their own right, and that it's not something to shy away from.

Neurodivergent individuals like me may face societal barriers, discrimination and misunderstanding when we seek to educate others and encourage a more balanced and positive approach. And as we know from sports, celebrity and the arts in general, the diversity that human beings bring to the table as individuals is what makes our species great and it's invaluable to be more inclusive as a society and look at this from a perspective of empowerment as opposed to focusing solely on deficits. Rather than being pathologized, neurodivergence is now being recognized as part of someone's identity, and that in and of itself is hugely valuable to cultivate within any culture or environment.

Myth 3: Neurodiversity promotes a one-size-fits-all approach

The neurodiversity movement champions individualized support and accommodation within the working environment, based on the unique strengths and challenges of each person, which means that we must consider the wide array of issues and mustn't become obsessed with trying to fix 'one big problem' rather than to consider how we might address individual needs through peer-to-peer support mechanisms or neurodiversity surveys where employees can address their needs as individuals.

Neurodiversity recognizes the diversity within the neurodivergent community. Each individual may have different sensory sensitivities, communication styles and preferences, so embracing neurodiversity means creating environments and support systems that allow for flexibility and customization, catering to the specific needs of each neurodivergent individual. This could consist of adopting technology, or providing software or hardware to cater for sensory needs or to increase an individual's ability to be productive; it could even be as simple as individualized coaching for those with ADHD to define structure, or a set of headphones for someone who has peaks of anxiety in loud environments.[2]

There are many simple and cost-effective solutions to cater for individual needs. However, many companies fail to do the relevant research aligned with staff that will help them create change. I often see this, even with disability – many companies focus on the ramps for wheelchair access, or things that seem more obvious, but they fail to ask what psychological support or adjustments might be needed for those with disabilities, because of their fear of causing offence, and many of my friends with seemingly traditional disabilities just want to be recognized as human beings in their own right and not have their organizations shy away from the discussion for fear of offending someone or not getting their terminology right.

Myth 4: Neurodiversity is limited to autism

For a long time, the term neurodiversity was used to signify autism. However, as I've touched on in previous chapters, neurodiversity should also cover conversations around diagnoses like Tourette's syndrome, epilepsy, dyslexia and bipolar disorder, among others. So, while autism is a prominent focus within the neurodiversity movement, it is essential to dispel the myth that neurodiversity is synonymous with autism alone. It fundamentally encompasses a broad spectrum of neurological variations.

As with anything diversity-related, each neurodivergent condition brings its own set of strengths and challenges, so it's paramount to recognize the diversity within neurodiversity, because this is crucial for fostering inclusivity and understanding the unique contributions of individuals with various neurological differences. Again, it comes back to considering and engaging with the individuals within an organization or society, so that we may better create awareness around individual needs.

Myth 5: Neurodiversity rejects treatment and support

Some believe that, because neurodiversity is about the neurological differences within individuals, the neurodiversity movement rejects treatment or support because it's down to individuals to adapt. However, this is not the case.[3]

Treatment and support are paramount to any individual who might struggle with their neurodivergence. With this in mind, the neurodiversity movement advocates for respectful and individualized support that aligns with the goals and preferences of the neurodivergent person in question, whether this be something that's offered within the workplace, or something that those individuals seek to find outside their vocational lives, through their doctors, psychologists or therapists.

While some neurodivergent individuals may choose to pursue therapies or interventions to address specific challenges, the neurodiversity paradigm questions the notion that all differences need to be 'fixed' or 'normalized'. It emphasizes the importance of autonomy and agency for neurodivergent individuals in making decisions about their own wellbeing.

I for one was told that I should take various medication to deal with my depressive episodes and anxieties. However, when I was diagnosed nearly 18 years ago, after trialling some medication and experiencing a detrimental impact on my cognitive functioning, I decided that if this was an issue that had been developed mentally, I was going to focus on psychological development to shift the balance in my favour. And to date I take no medication and have focused all my efforts on learning about my conditions and how to adapt and evolve myself on a mental and psychological basis to improve my day-to-day mindset/mental state and create a more sustainably happy lifestyle – and it's working! So, I am of the opinion that treatment and support should be offered and accessible, but should not be enforced, if the individual feels that they have the ability to cultivate their own means of introspection and self-development for the betterment of overarching mental resilience and adaptability.

Myth 6: Neurodivergent individuals lack empathy

This is probably one of the most common things that people consider and it's a persistent stereotype associated particularly with conditions like autism, where the general populace believe that neurodivergent individuals lack empathy. But the problem here is that this myth oversimplifies the complex ways in which individuals experience and express empathy. Neurodivergent individuals may have different social communication styles, but this does not equate to a lack of empathy; it just means that we very often express our feelings in different ways.

Research has shown that neurodivergent individuals often experience intense empathy, sometimes referred to as hyper-empathy. But, because individuals with conditions like autism often misinterpret non-verbal social cues, it is assumed that they must not have any empathy or depth of emotion; this is simply not the case. For those individuals like me, with neurodivergent conditions/traits, our capacity for empathy may be expressed in unique ways, such as a deep understanding of others' emotions or a strong sense of justice and fairness. I personally find it difficult to lie and I also have a wider level of anxiety when I feel like there is injustice, whether this be as simple as pranking a friend, or overlooking a person's needs or opinions in a working environment because of their perceived status. I also struggle if I feel someone is being bullied and have a strong need to rectify or speak out within these situations, to defend those who are abused, because somewhere in me I have an extreme and definitive sense of right and wrong. This is why I believe that to debunk the 'lack of empathy' myth is crucial for fostering understanding and dismantling stereotypes surrounding neurodiversity. We are all organisms who think and feel and while we may express that in different ways, it's nonetheless an important part of who we are, and it should be respected and treated as such.[4]

Myth 7: Neurodivergent individuals are unable to succeed in the workplace

Many workplaces and organizations shy away from championing neurodivergent leaders because the prevailing misconception is that we face insurmountable challenges in the workplace and are unable to succeed in various professional domains. However, this is a complete fiction, because neurodivergent individuals bring valuable skills and perspectives that can enhance workplace dynamics, as I explore throughout this book.

Diagnoses like autism, ADHD and dyslexia, while each is accompanied by their own set of challenges, are often associated with unique cognitive strengths, including pattern recognition, attention to detail and innovative thinking. Lots of neurodiverse employees excel in fields such as technology, mathematics and creative industries, and when championed are often seen as unique and irreplaceable assets.

With this in mind, I believe that companies who actively embrace neurodiversity in their workforce should ultimately recognize the benefits of diverse cognitive styles, because this fundamentally leads to increased innovation and problem-solving that could revolutionize your business.

Myth 8: Neurodiversity is a western concept

Mel Green from the Faculty of Wellbeing, Education and Language Studies at the Open University states, 'Some people believe that the neurodiversity concept is limited to western societies and does not resonate in other cultural contexts. But the reality is that the principles of neurodiversity are applicable globally, recognizing that neurological variations are present in all human populations. While ever changing and evolving terminology may vary, the essence of neurodiversity is a universal concept.

'The implication of the differences in value sets can be felt when diagnosing individuals. A lot of the diagnostic tools for assessing whether a person has a disability are based on Western norms. From a cultural approach, what is defined as "abnormal" will depend on expectations and standards of the society and the cultures the individuals belong to. For example, in some Asian and African communities, giving eye contact to an adult or to someone in authority is considered to be rude and children are actively taught not to do this. Yet, not maintaining eye contact is widely considered to be an autistic trait and something most, if not all, professionals will be looking out for when offering a diagnosis of autism.

'In the UK, it has been found that Asian school pupils (Indian, Pakistani, Bangladeshi and other Asian) are half as likely to be identified with autistic spectrum disorders as white British pupils. Linking this to the use of westernized diagnostics, it is possible to argue that cultural differences may explain this low incidence of Asian representation in the autistic community, as some of the features of these diagnostics are based on the norms for white British children and are not necessarily transferable to all children or young people.'[5]

Neurodivergent individuals exist in diverse cultural, ethnic and geographical contexts. This means that embracing neurodiversity requires acknowledging and respecting the cultural diversity within the neurodivergent community and adapting support strategies to align with cultural values and norms in a given region. However, it should not be the case that we as business leaders make assumptions that some countries or regions might be forfeit, or that the pursuit of better strategic initiatives surrounding neurodiversity should not be considered or developed, because this would be a critical error if you want to evolve as an organization on a global level.[6]

Myth 9: Neurodiversity is an excuse for poor behaviour

Probably more prevalent within the education system and schooling is the belief that neurodiversity is used as an excuse for poor behaviour, particularly in cases where individuals may exhibit social or communication challenges. But neurodivergent individuals, like anyone else, may encounter difficulties in navigating social interactions, and attributing such challenges solely to neurodiversity oversimplifies the complexities of human behaviour. Many children with ADHD, for example, are ruled out or under-recognized because they are seen as disruptive or naughty, but if you consider the context – that they may not be engaged in the same way as a neurotypical student or individual – then you can better assist their needs and drive their development and support systems to enhance their life in many ways, whether that be throughout their formative years in education, or within a workplace environment.

Individuals with varying neurodivergent traits may benefit from understanding and support in social situations, but it is essential to avoid using neurodiversity as a blanket excuse for poor behaviour, or to rule individuals with different needs out of certain activities or roles just because of a perceived potential threat to 'status quo'.

Myth 10: Neurodiversity is a fad

Some organizations shy away from addressing the needs of their neurodivergent staff because there is still a consideration that neurodiversity is a 'fad' or just a fleeting trend. However, as I mentioned previously, this is no different from considerations surrounding issues such as race or gender equality. It's merely a movement that seeks to gain the acknowledgement that we are all wired differently as individuals, and as such we all operate differently on a mental level. With this in mind, it should most definitely not be swept under the carpet as a fad or a fleeting area of interest when it comes to overarching workplace wellbeing. The pursuit of and a strategic approach to tackling sustainable support mechanisms surrounding neurodiversity both throughout education and within the world of work is something that needs to be taken seriously. Companies that fail to recognize this movement as a strategic imperative to the future development of their organization, culture and values will ultimately become dinosaurs in the future and will fail to attract the best talent when they try to expand and grow their businesses. We need to hire right and ensure an open mind and inclusive approach.

INSIGHT: The realities and myths of recruitment

Parul Singh is a highly successful neurodiversity consultant, recruitment expert, diverse female leader and public speaker. She is also a first-generation immigrant who has both an autism and ADHD diagnosis and has managed to carve her own path to success through adapting and evolving her understanding surrounding both her diagnosis and her intersectionality. Parul's inspiring career and experience to date is what made me keen to understand more about the realities that many will face when battling for traditional jobs, through stagnant recruitment processes. It's part of what I feel is paramount to understanding how companies can better avoid the neurodiversity myths and focus on the assets that hiring someone who is neurodiverse could bring to their business.

What's interesting about Parul's journey (but also quite common) is that she was misdiagnosed during the earlier part of her life, so I wanted initially to understand what she felt the difference was between how her traits impacted her back then and how she manages now in her adult life, after the clarity of finding the right diagnosis.

Parul told me, 'Before my diagnosis, I perceived my neurodivergent traits to be personality faults, as did the people around me. My ADHD and ASD traits caused a great deal of trauma growing up, which I am now having to face and process as an adult. But I learned that it's not possible to discipline neurodivergent traits out of myself, and that's why I struggled so much when I was younger because my teachers would just tell me to put effort into my homework and do it on time, and to focus more during lessons, which is near-impossible for someone with undiagnosed and unmanaged ADHD and ASD.'

Parul also noted that whilst ADHD medication has been a life-saver, she has observed two critical (and positive) mindset shifts in her life. 'Firstly, I give myself more self-compassion. I have accepted that I have a disability in some ways, and just as you can't tell someone in a wheelchair to just learn how to walk, you can't make someone with ADHD and ASD do things the way a neurotypical society wants them to. Secondarily, I realized why so many coping strategies and productivity methods didn't work for me, and with a deeper understanding of my mind I've been able to create my own strategies and coping mechanisms so that I can work with my ADHD and ASD instead of against them.'

Parul is also a strong advocate for companies developing their own internal employee resource groups (ERGs) and working with companies to set up their own neurodiverse leaders collectives internally. I was interested to understand why she feels so strongly that companies should be developing neurodiverse ERGs in the same vein, and how she would personally go about setting them up for success.

What Parul told me was that she is a big fan of the saying 'Nothing about us without us.' She stated, 'The reason so many organizations are not neurodivergent-friendly is because the people who make decisions about the way we work are doing it in the way that makes most sense for themselves as a neurotypical person. Neurodiversity ERGs create space for neurodivergent employees to influence and create positive change around policies and processes. It also creates a pathway for joining forces, and we need everyone to keep neurodivergence in mind in the workplace, so the advocacy work eventually becomes proactive as opposed to reactive (only changing things when they go wrong).'

At Parul's previous company, she founded and led the neurodiversity community ERG and in this role she was able to create a 'reasonable adjustments policy' and ensured there was a process when employees did disclose and request reasonable adjustments, such as I alluded to when discussing the myths surrounding neurodiversity. In addition to this, their Slack channel created a safe space for neurodivergent employees but also for neurotypical allies to share experiences, ask questions, learn from resources and much more.

Parul suggested that 'every organization is different but there are some key factors that can be crucial in defining the success of an ERG. One of the biggest challenges is getting buy-in. You need to have buy-in from the recruiting team and anyone involved in hiring. You need buy-in from HR, line managers, execs, the onboarding team, L&D, etc. as well as having an executive sponsor who will advocate for the ERG, because that's crucial for getting company-wide buy-in.

Another key factor would be focusing on making change where it's most beneficial for the specific organization. This could be the hiring process, promotion process, onboarding, training, etc. It's easy to want to immediately jump into everything but focusing on one area at a time and starting with the most critical is so important to sustainable change.'

I asked Parul whether she had any top tips for neurodivergent individuals looking for work and who are struggling to decide whether to be open about their diagnosis with new prospective employers. What was no surprise to me based on my personal experience working both for and with companies for nearly two decades was that Parul believes that 'disclosure is a privilege and not one that everyone can afford'. She told me, 'For neurodivergent people it always comes down to weighing up the risk vs reward when it comes to disclosure.

For most people the risk is higher during the interview process than it is when you're already in the workplace. As an ex-recruiter and someone who is neurodivergent myself, I will always advise people to assess the risks versus the reward using the following factors:

- How inclusive and progressive does the organization appear? Remember that sometimes it can be performative but sometimes it is possible to deduce based on what their employees post. Look out for insights on company blogs around changes they have actually made and the positive impact it's had; this is usually a good sign. If they have a diversity, equity and inclusion (DEI) statement with little substance or evidence of action and results, it may well just be lip service.

- Will disclosure and asking for reasonable adjustments remove barriers that make disclosure worth the risk? For example, if you're someone who is high masking and has coping mechanisms to manage through an interview process with adjustments and you fear the risk is too high, you may avoid disclosure.

- Are you in a position where you can use disclosure as a litmus test? If the organization does not respond positively to telling them you're neurodivergent then it's a good thing to find out sooner rather than later. This is often beneficial for people whose skills are in high demand and/or they are already in a job. Those applying for highly competitive roles and/or who are out of work may not be able to use this as a litmus test.

'After weighing up the risk and reward for your individual situation and jobs, you will be able to see whether disclosure and requesting reasonable adjustments is a net positive or a net negative.'

There is a lot of positive work being done around neurodiversity advocacy and a lot of companies really want to do the right thing but sometimes aren't sure how to approach it. By being confident and advocating for yourself you're giving yourself the best chance of success.

That being said, this chapter is also about the myths surrounding neurodiversity so I wanted to know from Parul what she felt were

some of the most common myths surrounding neurodivergent individuals that may make companies hesitant to give them a job. Her
response was that 'neurodivergent conditions are still quite misunderstood. As they are non-apparent disabilities, neurodivergent
people are often susceptible to ableism in the hiring process.
Employers need to understand that every neurodivergent person
comes with their own set of exceptional strengths, but these are
coupled with their own set of challenges in the workplace. Because of
certain negative coverage in the media, a lot of people still have incor-
rect assumptions about neurodivergent conditions. We're often
stereotyped, and interviewers can make their minds up about us
before we've even had a chance to prove ourselves.'

Some of the most common myths that Parul sees are 'that autistic
people are poor communicators, people with ADHD are disorgan-
ized or struggle to manage projects, that dyslexic people can't read or
write properly and that someone with Tourette's has a verbal tic
which causes them to swear uncontrollably – in fact, only 10 per cent
of people with Tourette's have a verbal tic.[7] Sometimes, employers
decide it's easier to avoid employing neurodivergent people than it is
to put in the work to support and understand them. That being said,
the return on investment is infinitely higher than the input from the
employer, so it makes business sense to bring in more neurodivergent
people to your business, but a big challenge is getting employers to
see the value in investing in hiring neurodivergent talent as a priority.'

Now, I mentioned that Parul was a first-generation immigrant,
with late-stage diagnoses for both autism and ADHD, but when we
spoke about this at the start of our interview process I was keen to
understand what Parul felt were the biggest obstacles that she had to
face on her road to becoming a successful diverse and neurodiverse
female leader.

One of the biggest challenges Parul mentioned was 'accepting my
neurodivergent traits and seeing them as a positive. I have so many
great qualities which I put down to being autistic and having ADHD.
However, growing up not knowing why I felt so different caused my
self-esteem and confidence to plummet, so the challenge comes in
undoing the harmful internal dialogue that I used to have with myself,

because that's been incredibly difficult, but the results now have proven to be very rewarding.'

Parul never advocated for herself, she perceived herself to be a 'nuisance' and was often told this by her teachers and friends, so she just learnt to get on with it. Becoming her best self-advocate has been a big barrier to overcome but it's clearly been critical to the success she's achieved so far in her career.

But should we always have to be so proactive when self-advocating? Or will we ever just be accepted as unique and different? I think it's probable that there needs to be a healthy mix of the two. As with most things in life. However, this led me to wondering whether Parul felt that companies are generally as ethical and impartial as they suggest when it comes to recruiting the right talent. Or whether she felt there's work to be done when it comes to diverse recruitment.

Her response was unsurprising but saddened me slightly. Parul was adamant that 'the majority of companies are not really as ethical as they suggest, because unfortunately a lot of it is performative and people still want to hire people who look, think and act like they do.

'Recruiters, particularly internal recruiters, hold a great deal of responsibility when it comes to creating accessible hiring processes. As someone who worked as an internal recruiter, I think that it's evident that the priorities are always focused on other things. Companies don't place enough emphasis on hiring diverse talent beyond a couple of lines on their job advert that says, "We welcome applicants from all backgrounds. Please ask us for reasonable adjustments if you need them."

'This means that traditional recruitment needs a massive overhaul, as it's not fit for purpose in most situations. For example, many companies still use psychometric tests when it's been proven to filter out neurodivergent candidates, and unless this archaic thinking and processing is modified for the needs of the workforce of today then companies will struggle to thrive as they could if they were more value-driven and dynamic in their approach.'

To be honest, while I've seen many of these issues first hand during my tenure in business, it was harrowing to hear from a young and established specialist in this field that there's not enough change moving at the pace we need to really break down the barriers, and there are still ignorant myths that stand in the way of those who are neurodivergent and their path to fulfilment within their careers.

Conclusion

My conclusion here is that debunking myths surrounding neurodiversity is essential for fostering a more inclusive and understanding society. By challenging these misconceptions, we can create environments that recognize and celebrate the diverse strengths and perspectives that neurodivergent individuals bring to the table.

Neurodiversity is not a trend but a fundamental shift in the way society perceives and values neurological differences. Acknowledging the complexities of neurodiversity, understanding individual needs and promoting inclusivity can contribute to a world where neurodivergent individuals are empowered to thrive in all aspects of life, free from the constraints of misinformation and stigma.

So, perhaps by educating ourselves a little both on an individual leader level and on an organizational level as businesses, we might better understand how to embrace the people we meet in our lives every day that could be diverse for a whole wealth of different reasons. Most people evolve only based on what they know, and it is our ignorance of things or lack of learning new things that holds us back, so my hope is that not only this chapter but the entirety of my book will serve to change that in some small way by make people less ignorant when it comes to how they perceive neurodiversity.

Notes

1 J Harris. The mother of neurodiversity: How Judy Singer changed the world, *The Guardian*, 5 July 2023. www.theguardian.com/world/2023/jul/05/the-mother-of-neurodiversity-how-judy-singer-changed-the-world (archived at https://perma.cc/3VDS-5RGQ)

2 A Thornburrow. Embracing neurodiversity: One size really doesn't fit all, Salveson Mindroom Centre, 13 January 2023. www.mindroom.org/alan-thornburrow-embracing-neurodiversity-one-size-really-doesnt-fit-all/ (archived at https://perma.cc/3ANR-G3WX)

3 R Dean (2018) Neurodiversity and the rejection of cures, in A Cureton and T E Hill, Jr (eds), *Disability in Practice: Attitudes, policies, and relationships*, Oxford Academic, Oxford

4 D Sullivan. Autistic people don't lack empathy. In fact, we've got more than enough, Neurodiverging, 2023. www.neurodiverging.com/autistic-people-dont-lack-empathy-in-fact-weve-got-more-than-enough/ (archived at https://perma.cc/A87M-XQU2)

5 M Green. Neurodiversity: What is it and what does it look like across races? Open University, September 2020. www.open.edu/openlearn/health-sports-psychology/mental-health/neurodiversity-what-it-and-what-does-it-look-across-races (archived at https://perma.cc/P6XX-W94U)

6 M McCune. How does culture guide our understanding of neurodiversity? B-RAD Lab, 9 January 2024. www.b-radlab.com/news/how-does-culture-guide-our-understanding-of-neurodiversity (archived at https://perma.cc/HPU7-5M9X)

7 M Freeman-Ferguson. Tourette's syndrome: Challenging misconceptions and improving understanding, Nursing Children and Young People, 1 September 2022. pubmed.ncbi.nlm.nih.gov/35312241/ (archived at https://perma.cc/PHH5-5TDJ)

PART TWO

Empowering your business

4

Harnessing neurodivergence

I hope that it is clear to readers at this point that neurodiversity, the recognition and celebration of neurological differences, has the potential to revolutionize both personal lives and businesses. By embracing diverse cognitive styles and perspectives, individuals and organizations can unlock innovation, creativity and resilience. My exploration in this chapter delves into how harnessing neurodivergent thinking can lead to transformative changes in various aspects of life and business, so I wanted to explore the benefits, challenges and practical strategies for individuals and businesses looking to leverage neurodiversity.

First of all, we need to evolve our understanding of neurodivergent thinking, by which I mean cognitive processes and perspectives that deviate from the neurotypical norms. Neurodivergent individuals often exhibit unique thinking patterns, problem-solving approaches and sensory perceptions. Recognizing and valuing these differences, whether you want to harness or cultivate individuals within a business or are looking to understand yourself following a neurodiversity diagnosis, can lead to a multitude of benefits both at an individual level and within the organizational context.

We know that neurodivergent individuals often bring a fresh and innovative approach to problem-solving. Their ability to think in an unconventional way can lead to groundbreaking ideas and solutions, and so it's evident that businesses that tap into this creativity gain a competitive edge in an ever-evolving marketplace. But, in addition, when we consider that neurodivergent thinking is characterized by diverse cognitive strengths such as pattern recognition, attention to detail and specialized skills, we can better understand that these strengths contribute to more comprehensive problem-solving strategies, enabling individuals and teams to navigate a wide range of complex business and social challenges effectively.

It's also important to recognize that neurodiverse people's attention to detail is heightened, which is a quality that is invaluable in various professions, including technology, research and quality assurance, because it brings clarity of thinking and judgement. What's more, it's instinctual, so when cultivated and channelled this meticulous approach can lead to improved accuracy and precision in tasks that need strategic insight and proactive measures that come off the back of calculated risk.[1]

Everything about cultivating neurodiversity in business also relates back to companies' need to foster a culture of diversity and inclusion. Neurodiversity brings with it a range of diverse perspectives with a breadth of context. Different perspectives in life and business enrich discussions, leading to well-rounded decision-making and a more innovative approach to business strategies when you are not only considering the blue skies thinking, but when you're looking to break down the problem and structure deliverables in a manageable way, to ensure key performance indicators are met and that tasks are completed efficiently and effectively within controlled timeframes and budgets.

One of the aspects that people consistently underestimate about neurodiverse leaders or individuals is our resilience and adaptability. And what rises to the surface is a consistent assumption that we might be mentally weak, or strained, or unstable, when in reality, because we have had to endure a diagnosis that effectively defines what might be considered 'a disorder', neurodivergent individuals often develop resilience and adaptability as a result of navigating a world that may not always accommodate their differences. And it is this resilience that can be a hugely valuable asset in the face of change and uncertainty, contributing to personal and professional success. This steadfast adaptability is a trait that any good business would wish to cherish in their employees, regardless of their area of specialization.

INSIGHT: Harnessing neurodivergent thinking

For this chapter, I spoke to Lee Chambers, a prominent black business leader and renowned psychologist, to get his take on the best avenues for harnessing neurodivergent thinking. One of the most interesting aspects about Lee is that he was a qualified psychologist, supporting people clinically to evolve and change, before he was diagnosed with being on the autism spectrum only a few years ago.

Lee has fought to stand apart from the crowd his whole life, always knowing he was different, tackling challenges with not just his mental health, but also because of issues surrounding intersectionality along the way. So, I wanted initially to understand more about what he thinks is the biggest failing with regards to allyship in the workplace wellbeing agenda, not specifically in reference to neurodiversity but in the context of looking at diversity as a whole.

So, in addition to some of what I covered with Lee, here are the four pillars, as I see them, that will help to underpin the right values/culture for engaging, cultivating and safeguarding your neurodivergent staff.

Social misunderstandings

We need to remember that neurodivergent individuals may experience challenges in social interactions, leading to misunderstandings and potential isolation. Therefore, it's imperative that in addressing these challenges you're looking to foster a culture of understanding and providing support for diverse communication styles. This links back to evolving your leadership training, keeping line managers nimble and educated, and being aware that tempering or modifying your flexible working structures could dramatically increase productivity for the neurodiverse and remove some of the anxiety that comes with too much rigidity or social overwhelm.

Lee stated, 'Wellbeing in itself is quite a privilege, to be able to be in a place where you can actively work on that. The other big issue within the industry is the tendency to overlook the diverse needs and experiences of people from marginalized and minoritized groups, who face systemic inequality, discrimination and sometimes even oppression, because that also has a significant impact on wellbeing and creates a very unique set of challenges faced by certain individuals based on the intersections that they fall into.'

He also suggested, 'We have a tendency in workplace wellbeing to think that everyone's starting from the same start line, and it's simply not the case. This is why a blanket approach to wellbeing won't create engagement and doesn't create sustainable change. And because of this context it's become ever more important to really look at how we foster cultures of belonging and psychological safety, because if you do feel valued, you're more likely to get to the prescribed start line, or to be able to access what's available already. You might think, "How can we get Thomas the support to get to where he needs to go, from his respective base point?" It's only this that will give companies and individuals the ability to thrive, off the back of these unique perspectives, talents, individuals and contributions.'

Sensory sensitivities

When it comes to sensory sensitivities, these issues are quite common among neurodivergent individuals, and they can obviously pose challenges in certain environments. With this in mind, by creating sensory-friendly spaces and implementing accommodations your business can help to mitigate these difficulties for the individuals challenged. But we also need to consider the depth of emotions within certain individuals based on their experience and personal journey.

One of the problems Lee is challenged by is that the empathy and sensitivity in his mind is not always apparent on his face or in the most typical ways, but it's true in his head in quite an amplified way. This makes him effective in many senses, but it requires an active approach to harnessing and controlling this issue so that it is channelled, because if that sort of thing isn't channelled then he feels it would be more of a blocker to being effective.

Lee's hyper-focus and productivity can also get him into a scenario where he can achieve quite a lot in a very short space of time. However, this can also be detrimental if he lets it overshadow the variety of other things. He stated, 'I need to be doing to keep my brain happy because I can go too deep into things. As a result, this is another aspect to my neurodiversity that needs channelling, because if I let it get out of control then I will work for 17 or 18 hours and on the other side of those efforts my overarching wellbeing can fall by the wayside.'

It's obvious that Lee's lack of conformity of thinking creates issues in strategic areas because, as he suggested to me, 'people can't see things from my perspective or struggle to get a grip on understanding the nuances of my thought process, but on the other side of the coin I've been able to balance this strategic thinking, against things like my really strong pattern recognition, with my acute attention to detail and most people only have one or the other trait, so doing both of these things quite intensely means it helps me to engage people in joining up the dots.'

Lee also believes that his dedication to and passion for what he does vocationally helps to maintain stability when channelling the aforementioned hyper-focus and productivity because, for him, it's 'like a source of justice and I can utilize this to contest systems, utilizing my disruptive soul to bring foresight and clarity to the table for others. But I admit that this capacity to harness neurodivergence is due to becoming older and wiser, and when you're younger it's often very difficult to understand how to channel your instincts or sensitivities in the most productive capacity.'

Stigma and stereotypes

If I were going back into the world of work today, as opposed to running my own business, I would have to recognize that stigma and stereotypes surrounding neurodivergent conditions persist in society and therefore this bleeds readily into vocational endeavours. It is therefore paramount that consistent and sustainable education and awareness initiatives are employed readily because this wider level of communication is essential, if we are to dispel any myths and foster a more inclusive mindset throughout our businesses. We need to change the narrative and this only comes with consistency in our approach to awareness and inclusion.

What Lee suggested is that 'there is a very clear lack of intersectional understanding and action in workplace wellbeing across the board. I believe that in the wellbeing space itself, those that are creating products and services and those that are building the strategies are generally doing that from a place of privilege, and there are many things they don't really see or consider when those strategies, products or services are being built/designed.

'We should more deeply consider those aspects of discrimination and oppression; the feeling that you don't belong, or the feeling like you're not included in wellbeing because there's a barrier to even accessing it in the first place, given that you're probably starting from a different "wellbeing equity" perspective, further from the start line than some other people in your workplace.'

What I thought was most interesting about Lee's comments surrounding allyship and intersectionality in the context of wellbeing was that we are actually all starting our wellbeing journey from different points on the racetrack, and in fact the comment that struck a chord was that 'Some people are actually starting their wellbeing race outside of the stadium!'

I can definitely empathize with this message and mindset, because it's inherently similar to much of what I've faced throughout my life, in the context of feeling segregated at school or within work environments because I operate on a different stream of energy, especially in some environments where I was the poor kid competing against the posh boys for visibility and credibility. I was also keen to understand how Lee felt he was further marginalized as a black man when it came to his vocational endeavours further down the line and how he was able to tip the balance in his favour to become such an effective and respected diverse leader.

What Lee explained to me was that 'I look at this from two aspects of my journey, as well as what I have since learned from others with a similar background. But as a black man you are more likely to be inherently perceived as a criminal, and as a young black male you are not necessarily going to be aware of that. You only start to notice this sort of thing when, for example, people cross the road when you're walking down the street, and other little things like this. But, fundamentally, it also means that you miss out on things like the opportunity to be diagnosed, and you're more likely to be labelled as a troublemaker or disruptive, or the assumption is made that your parents probably won't really care, so there's no communication when it comes to either flagging needs, or even getting help and support.'

When Lee was older and went into the world of work, he said that he 'believes that the environment just didn't really work for me, for several reasons, but I believe this was probably more due to my neurodiversity than my ethnicity. Ultimately you are who you are and there comes a point where you can't worry about how others perceive you because you have to crack on. I've done that by building my own businesses and running those effectively, while building a support network around me to help with the things I'm not good at and to mitigate some of the factors that come with navigating the corporate world through various intersections.' So, Lee believes that all of this has an impact, but a lot is about how you tackle it as an individual and avoid allowing it to swallow you up or make you resentful or bitter. He also said, 'You have additional stereotypes laid upon you because of elements outside your control, like the amount of black men that end up in the prison system, or with my not getting a diagnosis and people assuming that I may just be an angry black man as opposed to someone battling with understanding how to manage various issues that could have been channelled earlier given access to a diagnosis.'

Drilling a bit deeper into his personal experience, I was also keen to understand more readily how Lee himself took what many may consider a difficult diagnosis and turn it into a positive to improve his life as an individual. Lee told me that as he 'reflected and thought about how I felt at the point of diagnosis, and the best way I could describe it was that it is part partially liberating and partially frightening.

'It's so important that firstly we understand that at the point of diagnosis everyone is going to have a whole range of emotions. There is no perfect way to take a diagnosis and just roll with it, because for some there will be a hell of a lot more unpicking, more challenges to their identity, more things that they have to navigate to get to a place where they are happy and able to look forward, because there's lots of work to be done.'

What Lee suggested had worked for him was 'focusing on being able to harness the power of feeling unleashed, but also to work through feeling scared and frightened and feeling like you just want to stand still.' And for Lee this meant 'working on self-acceptance because while I had to do some internal work on myself, I also had to accept that while I may have only just received a diagnosis, that fundamentally this reality had always been the case and I knew I must set about working on gaining some forgiveness for some of the things I've done in my life and some of the aspects of my journey where I had beaten myself up a bit.' He told me that he had to look at the things he wasn't proud of quite objectively and acknowledge that there were other things at play that he didn't realize until now, because while he'd always known he was different, he simply never knew why.

Moving forward with this way of thinking, Lee feels that he 'fostered an element of actively working on the understanding around it, as well as what it all meant in the bigger picture and what it meant for me. So, what I'm suggesting is that the time to reflect and start to understand myself a little bit gave me an extra sense of empowerment to move away from the difficulty, toward the feeling that I could take control and harness some of the diverse aspects to the way I did things, and this led me to getting a clearer picture as to how I could really capitalize on the strengths I have as an individual.'

Lee had always known that there were certain things that he was 'far more effective at than the average human being', but he also had issues where friends couldn't understand how things that may seem simple to the 'average' person just baffled him. He couldn't understand how he could do certain things so effectively and those other elements would bring him to his knees. He suggested that 'it gave me a feeling of autonomy to go and capitalize on the strengths that I'd recognized in myself and in focusing on them I truly understood the value that I could bring to others. I also recognized that the way I learned to do this more effectively was through my connections with others, because I would go into relationships embracing new elements to my identity and build the types of relationships that would have more depth, and those were the sort of relationships that would sustain me through difficult times. Because I was focused on people who engaged in my strength areas, I had a diverse range of perspectives to draw on but they helped me navigate my life and who I wanted to be with a level of stability when I was feeling more volatile or challenged internally.'

Lee believes that the mentality of evolving how you are growing as an individual and growing professionally is underpinned by your ability to contribute to others, because that helps you to continue to refine what you can do, while defining who you are and at the same time feel like your presence makes an active and purposeful difference in the world; and this ability to contribute will again become like a layer of protectiveness against the inner critic in you, telling you you're not good enough. This is ultimately why we can move the needle for more individuals or across business landscapes if we try to remove stigma and set aside historic stereotyping that could hinder perception and devalue our human assets.

Lee went on to tell me that, as an individual, 'if you want others to show up and you are in a position where you sadly have to try to minimize the potential of being stereotyped, then you have to develop an internal code that defines you turning up in a certain way, or minimizing certain aspects of yourself, as a fundamental for survival, so that you don't end up in those boxes, because those boxes are not good for a neurodivergent and they're not good for any diverse individual.' The other aspect he believes is that he must focus heavily on being inclusive himself; 'being willing to sit there and listen to people who've got views that trigger you, because otherwise you can't expect people on the other side who see you as completely different, to also do that. This is where allyship comes in, because you've got to create space to listen to the differences in people and their background, you've got to build a diverse network of people and be open to challenge and not always follow the party line if it doesn't make sense.'

Access to opportunities

It's very common for neurodivergent individuals to face barriers when seeking educational and employment opportunities. It's a shame, but it's a reality. This means that it is imperative that proactive measures, such as neurodiversity hiring initiatives, are defined and implemented to better address these disparities, as well as continued education surrounding accessibility to roles and opportunities for progressive development on an individualistic level.

But what about businesses looking to promote allyship and neurodiversity in tangent? If you are a people, HR or business leader looking to move the needle, then I feel that Lee's top tips for businesses looking to promote allyship and neurodiversity as part of their cultural evolution towards more sustainable and effective workplace wellbeing should be considered carefully as cornerstones for improvement.

Lee's biggest want for companies is to 'focus on engagement in inclusion and wellbeing, because I believe that you've got to make it actually feel like it's something people can take part in. Historically with inclusion a lot of men feel like there's nothing in it for them and that being open is reducing their opportunities, so a big part of your approach as a business is actually changing hearts and minds by showcasing how collaborative this process of inclusion can be; but you also need to measure progress and impact along the way.'

Currently inclusion and wellbeing are under attack because a lot of businesses are not seeing the impact or the difference it's making to individuals, which means they won't keep funding it and it won't be sustainable. So, this measured impact must be defined and seen.

Another fundamental that Lee mentioned is around 'promoting allyship and advocacy internally. Instead of creating this massive competition backed environment where everyone is pitted against each other, we need to try to get people to step back and think about how supporting others can actually increase their ability, can add to their personal skillset and make them better leaders, but most businesses have such poorly backed resource groups and networks that they fail to use them effectively. So marginalized groups need to be resourced properly and not just with one group, but with everyone, to truly use them for the power they have. If you fund initiatives properly and encourage the groups to collaborate together, to see those intersections and bring those intersections to life, then you will evoke vast and sustainable change.'

Lee believes it's also evident that every business needs to 'look at recruitment and hiring practices, as well as how you retain talent. Wellbeing is a huge part of that, especially for the next generation of business leaders. Those individuals coming into your workplace in the future are not going to put up with poor workplace conditions; they'll be asking questions like "What do you do here?" and "What's the culture like?" And they won't want you to tell them, they will want you to show them!

'Education and awareness cannot always be measured at the start of a journey, but it is paramount to get people to understand what it is, what it looks like and how it can be tailored to them, so if you get managers, for example, to be part of personalizing these things and ensure that the managers have the capacity to role model it them-selves and the capability and competence to do that, then you're winning. Making sure that leaders are committed when they are brought into the discussions and strategies, and that everyone across the business is responsible for driving these values and practices forward.'

Advice for people struggling to come to terms with a diagnosis

Aside from these four pillars, as a psychologist, part of Lee's chosen vocation even before being diagnosed was to help other people to understand themselves and stabilize their lives on a psychological level, neurodivergent or otherwise, but what I was also interested to understand from him was what advice he would give to others on the autism spectrum who are struggling to come to terms with their diag-nosis and what that means for their day-to-day lives.

He told me that 'in reflecting on this question, a lot of the stuff that I did for myself would most definitely be the things I would suggest as things for other people to try, outside of also seeking a support network and connecting socially with others, to build confidence in communication and community.'

Lee suggested that 'while it's important to work to educate yourself from differing sources when it comes to understanding your personal neurodiversity, it's also important not to hyper-focus on it too much, so that you can gain a balanced approach to widening your perspective on what your diagnosis is and what it actually means to you, and consider what it might mean for the future.'

His concern in part was that we've got such a such a variety of sources available now, whether that be people sharing what their journey is like from a lived experience perspective on TikTok, to those that have been researching it for 50 years, and that 'there's so much information out there that sometimes it's about how you pick up those little nuggets from so many diverse areas without thinking that anyone knows one version of the truth, because everyone's journey and understanding is unique.'

Lee is of the firm belief that 'the only real version of truth is the one that you experiment with yourself, but for me it always loops back to tapping in again to focus on your strengths in those periods. If you consistently try to practise self-compassion, you become more effective at communicating your needs to other people, without feeling guilty for doing so and that then helps create the ecosystem around you that is more supportive, because while people get clarity on what you need you can proactively ask for it without feeling like you are putting a lot of strain on others, in part because you've got that clarity and you understand the impact it has on you.'

Another thing he found soothing was 'to have some kind of flexible vision for the future and some realistic goals, that will serve you as stepping stones moving towards that vision. If you're struggling to come to terms with it and you don't have any clarity on what the future might hold, you very often get stuck there, in this sort of "sinking sand" mindset; but if you can form a flexible vision, or maybe even look at redefining a little bit of what success actually means to you now, from a slightly different perspective, and set some kind of realistic goals within that plan, you suddenly get a structure to work to and that structure gives you a level of stability and reliability, which is something most neurodivergent individuals need.'

Lee classifies these thought processes as anchors that 'hold you in the tides of overwhelm' along the way, as you find your feet exploring coping strategies that are going to work for you as an individual, because it's hard to explore coping strategies when everything feels really volatile and uncertain and you know there's complexity around you, whereas it's easier to explore coping strategies if you feel anchored and you've got a base structure to maintain you.

The other thing that had helped him was simply to 'try to ask people to just embrace your identity, as you would for yourself. For a lot of autistic individuals, you have limits on how you can express yourself, so for me it's how I dress, or my funky glasses, my sense of style, and while there are lots of potential ways, this has helped me to be grounded and to find myself and feel more like I know myself as I approach the world every day.'

It is often said that if you can harness your neurodivergent traits, you can become far more effective in both your working life and your personal life, so part of my intrigue for interviewing Lee as someone both on the autism spectrum and in the field of psychology, was to explore his thoughts on this.

Lee's take on this concept is, 'Firstly my neurodiversity is what makes me stand out as an individual, that's what makes me, me. Because of this I have a degree of empathy and sensitivity that really helps when it comes to coaching or the interpersonal work that I do with my clients and it helps me to foster difficult and courageous conversations.'

His neurodivergence also helps him to 'appreciate and embrace people's differences and to talk with people about different perspectives and beliefs, rather than simply jumping to make a judgement about them.' However, he made it clear that he does have to fight elements of his own kind in the doing. His perfectionism often holds him back, for example, but in the context of communication Lee feels that he has 'found a nice balance where people feel like they are being listened to' when he's engaging with them.

Referring back to his time at school, Lee suggested that he 'didn't really put much effort in'. So he did pretty well academically, especially with the areas that were of interest to him, where he applied himself; however, he often ended up in the head teacher's office, only to be told that they'd never met a student who could so well articulate why certain elements of the education system simply didn't interest him, or detail the journey that led to him being there in the first place. Often this capacity for assertive and clear thinking would get him out of trouble along the way and afford him the ability to forge his own process for education in spite of being disenfranchised. Lee noted that 'in the earlier stages the teachers I battled with often ended up having a degree of respect for my capacity to argue my case, and this led to my becoming friends with a number of teachers, which then gave me some stability in maintaining my courses to completion and success, but it was all a balancing act and an opportunity for me to test out who I was and how I fitted within the spectrum of the world and systems that surrounded me.'

It's obvious to me that Lee feels lucky that he has been able to become successful in his own field of interest, because it has enabled him to stay on the right side of things for a long time and even led to him being able to get a diagnosis at 36 years old. But when he ponders on what he has done to tip the balance in his favour it comes down to his ability to advocate for himself a lot, learn how to speak up for himself and how to challenges others in a way that didn't amplify the perceived threat of being a black man already.

He mentioned that he put a post on LinkedIn about his funky glasses and that 'as soon as you wear glasses as a black person you look a bit more of an intellectual and a bit less of a threat. Little things like this have given me the ability to get into deeper conversations and not to be torn down straight away.'

When Lee dropped out of university while struggling, he realized his biggest learning to date is that 'you can continue your professional development in addition to personal introspective development even without having a traditional framework, course or academic institution behind you. And this gives you an edge, while it also gives you purpose and meaning, so you don't fall into this pit of defining yourself by a pre-prescribed society standard or assumption of who you are or who you are expected to become.'

The other point he feels is paramount is 'building that network and getting eyes on you and what you're about, because it's really easy to focus lots of work on yourself, or lots of work trying to influence others, and the problem is that you either end up really good at what you do, but no one knows who you are, or everyone knows who you are, but no one knows that you continue to develop and grow, or fully understands what it is that you do.' So, Lee has had to use those two pillars, which he terms the 'interpersonal/one-on-one relationship and the outer ecosystem', building lots of knowledge within different systems and simultaneously leading by example, but remembering to lead yourself first.

The competitive advantage of neurodiversity

From my perspective as I write this book, I think that, before delving into more depth on how to harness neurodivergent thinking, it's also crucial to me that we address the challenges and misconceptions that persist. In acknowledging these issues, individuals and businesses can work towards creating environments that support and capitalize on neurodiversity as part of both their DEI strategies and their wider workplace wellbeing agenda.

Neurodiversity should be seen not as a hindrance to business but clearly as a competitive advantage. And in individuals harnessing their neurodivergent traits, or companies empowering employees to thrive and become the best of themselves, we will only see value off the back of this both in business and in our wider society. Wired Consulting did a great piece with Alison Kay, Managing Partner at EY, to look at why neurodiversity is good for business. EY actively recruits individuals that deem themselves to have what EY call neuro-cognitive differences and it's refreshing to see more and more companies waking up to this concept as we evolve our thinking surrounding innovation and the evolution of how our businesses and employee ecosystems operate.[2]

Key strategies for individuals: Unlock your potential

Now, perhaps you're reading this book as an individual and you are looking to tackle a recent diagnosis, or maybe you simply wish to harness your thinking as a neurodivergent person and get a little introspective? I would therefore suggest several steps you can take to unlock your potential and contribute meaningfully to your personal and professional lives.

The following are elements that I have employed to ensure a more sustainably happy lifestyle and reduce my level of day-to-day anxiety given my variety of diagnoses:

- **Self-acceptance and advocacy**: The first part of any individual journey begins with self-acceptance. Embracing your neurodivergent identity and recognizing your unique strengths is crucial. Individuals can and should most definitely engage in self-advocacy, articulating their needs and preferences in various contexts, so don't shrink in the face of a diagnosis – embrace it.

- **Build a support system**: Surrounding yourself with a supportive network, including friends, family and mentors, or even engaging with a neurodiversity coach or therapist, can provide emotional support and guidance. Connecting with neurodivergent communities and advocacy groups will also offer you a platform for shared experiences and insights, which will help you to navigate both your life and vocational challenges, as they arise.

- **Identify your strengths and passions**: One thing that is paramount is recognizing your individual strengths and passions, because this allows you to channel your energy into areas where you can excel. And this self-awareness will help you to form the basis for personal and professional growth.

- **Develop your communication and collaboration skills**: Developing effective communication and collaboration skills is crucial for navigating social and professional environments, so I wholeheartedly encourage this, even though sometimes it might feel alien. Seeking opportunities for skills development, such as workshops or mentorship/coaching programmes, can enhance your abilities and will galvanize your self-worth, building trust in who you are as a human being, and if we know ourselves then we can truly evolve.

- **Leverage technology and tools:** Don't be afraid to embrace technology or assistive tools, because they can be powerful allies for us as neurodivergent individuals. From apps that support organization and time management to communication aids, leveraging available tools can enhance your productivity and efficiency, help you to avoid procrastination and channel your energy.

Key strategies for organizations: Create the right environment

With the above in mind, I thought it worthwhile to widen the detail surrounding key strategies for organizations in creating environments that capitalize on neurodiversity. This will help business leaders with a step-by-step approach to ensuring you've covered the eight fundamental bases where I often see businesses failing:

- **Inclusive hiring practices:** Implementing inclusive hiring practices involves creating a neurodiversity-friendly recruitment process. This includes providing alternative interview formats, ensuring accessible application processes and educating hiring teams about neurodivergent strengths and potential.

- **Training and awareness programmes:** Conducting training programmes for employees on neurodiversity fosters a more inclusive workplace culture. Awareness initiatives can dispel myths, reduce stigma and promote understanding of neurodivergent conditions. It couldn't hurt to give all your line managers a copy of this book, for example, as a starting point, but sustainable and regular training and engagement are necessary in the long term.

- **A flexible work environment:** Creating a flexible work environment accommodates the diverse needs of neurodivergent individuals. This includes considerations for sensory sensitivities, offering flexible work hours and providing designated quiet spaces.

- **Mentorship programmes:** Establish mentorship programmes that pair neurodivergent employees with mentors who can provide guidance and support. Mentors can offer insights into navigating the workplace and help neurodivergent individuals develop their professional skills. This is something that is commonly missed in businesses, but it's easy to implement and will dramatically increase productivity, especially when senior leadership show their support by joining the mentoring process.

- **Accessible professional development:** Adapting professional development opportunities to be accessible and inclusive is essential. Tailoring training programmes to accommodate diverse learning styles ensures that neurodivergent individuals can engage meaningfully in continuous learning. You must also remember that around 20 per cent of your workforce will be neurodivergent, whether they've been diagnosed or not, so advancement in dynamic training processes will likely add value to those you might not even be aware needed it.

- **Neurodiversity employee resource groups:** Forming neurodiversity ERGs (much like my Neurodiverse Leaders Collective that I set up for my clients) within the organization provides a platform for networking, sharing experiences and advocating for neurodivergent individuals. These groups can contribute to a sense of community and inclusion. They can also act as a 'think tank' where you can utilize people's diverse thinking to gain innovations and insights that might revolutionize your business in ways you never thought possible.

- **Leadership commitment:** Leadership commitment to neurodiversity initiatives is crucial for any business and its success. When leaders prioritize and champion diversity and inclusion, it sets the tone for the entire organization and promotes a culture that values neurodivergent thinking.

- **Accommodations and support systems:** Implementing accommodations and support systems ensures that neurodivergent individuals have the resources they need to thrive. This may include flexible work arrangements, assistive technologies and personalized support plans. While this may take different forms, depending on your industry or type of business, it's a worthwhile endeavour that will add huge value to your people and teams.

INSIGHT: Good practice at a major automobile company

In order to learn a bit more about what businesses who are more well known have been doing to support, acknowledge and champion their neurodivergent staff, I talked to Matt Loynes, who has been working at Ford Motor Company for over two decades.

Identifying as autistic, Matt has spent the last five years of his multi-decade tenure at the industry goliath heading up and managing a team who jump in and out of different projects across the company to innovate and offer insights into where things can be developed and improved to ensure success. What is unique in this circumstance is that the company have clearly recognized that Matt's brain works differently and that he is loyal to the brand and its success, so they have given him the support to utilize that creative and innovative mind for the betterment of his career and the brand, as they evolve.

Initially, one of the things I was keen to know from Matt was, as someone who identifies as autistic, what did he feel had been the biggest challenge when it came to him building such a successful career to date? He told me, 'One of the most important challenges I had to tackle, was and is knowing myself and my triggers.' Matt believes that 'acceptance has a big part to play as well, and that only comes through life experience and understanding who you are as a whole. Looking back, I didn't realize that not everyone had the same level of stress and anxiety that I have every day, dealing with the world, let alone my work. I was often told, "You're not stressed" or You're not overloaded" by other individuals and I found that a massive challenge and hindrance, because I was always then trying to mirror neurotypical responses and didn't even realize I was doing it, or forming a mask, to fit in. And this issue was impacting my very state of being.'

Matt also mentioned that 'there were also issues surrounding unconscious bias from teams using such terms as "We are all neuro-diverse, we know how it feels" and "I'm sure you can do it." Which made me feel even more inadequate throughout my career, and this was something I had to chip away at over time.'

That being said, he was still ushered into this innovative role off the back of his neurodivergent strength, so I asked him why he thinks that neurodiverse individuals are more effective when it comes to looking at company innovation. His response was that 'innovation by its nature is about challenging the status quo and looking for a new approach to an existing or potential issue, and companies need to find a plain where neurodivergent individuals have the potential to thrive off the back of how we see the world and deal with it on a daily basis. Companies will always benefit from an unfiltered response, and you might want a range of "outlandish" ideas so that you can pinpoint what might help you thrive. You need as a business in a competitive market to want someone to ask "Why?" and this is what you can achieve with a diverse group of individuals when it comes to innovation. Divergence is a key tenet of innovation, and I believe firmly that without it you cannot deliver a robust convergence of ideas and thoughts that stretch a given concept to it true potential.'

What is interesting to me is that many individuals who are neuro-divergent jump around a little over the years, or run their own businesses, in order not to be caged by protocol or hindered by red tape when decision-making, but Matt has been a solid employee of arguably one of the biggest brands in the world for nearly 24 years. So, I was keen to understand how he had become so effective in busi-ness and maintained such a tenure with the automotive giant while dealing with the challenges surrounding his neurodivergence. What's interesting is that Matt said, 'For much of my career I had been hiding in plain sight. Fitting in, not rocking the boat. Trying to balance the challenges of work to the expense of my life outside of work. And operating like this is just simply not sustainable if you want to fully embrace life and who you are as an individual.'

He suggested that 'it was actually through the support of several mentors, I came to the realization that I needed to be myself and not to hide who I was if I was to thrive. Yet I do still hide in plain sight to a degree, but now I am simply much more open about who I am and why I make certain decisions or think in a certain way.' Matt told me that 'finding a role that allows me to be myself and bring my best self to work every day, has been the single biggest challenge for me throughout my career and it's becoming slightly easier now that I truly know who I am and I don't feel so alone, because the younger generation is coming into the world of business with a very different outlook and they are much more open about their diagnosis and who they are, which makes it easier for me to feel at ease with my way of operating.'

Another thing that always concerns me, and something I was keen to gain Matt's insights on, was where he felt that big businesses are generally failing when it comes to tackling neurodiversity as part of their wider workplace wellbeing and culture initiatives. And in response to this Matt told me that 'it's so often a prevalent attitude that we must adapt or die, and the same is true within big businesses, often missing the mark when it comes to looking after people's needs. It's that mindset of "This is how we've always done things" in many companies and that just doesn't serve them to evolve. As business leaders and company leaders we must strive to create a working environment where you can bring your whole self to work without the fear of persecution or repercussions, and companies need to become more understanding, creating a culture where the whole person is valued and nurtured to be the best that they can be and thrive as an individual. But my mindset is that this can only work if companies bring together traditional skills training, in tangent with wellbeing, diversity, equity and inclusion where at the root there's an understanding that everyone has unique skills they could bring to the business if given the opportunity and scope to do so.'

So, clearly there were challenges for Matt over the years, but he's still been supported in many ways by his company as his career has progressed, and with that in mind I wanted to know how the brand had empowered Matt as an individual to thrive so readily within their business, for the betterment of the company? And what made him decide to devote himself to the brand for so many years?

Being candid, he told me it was a bit of a difficult question because 'in the early stages it started out that I was a little fearful of change and there was a resounding feeling of comfort in being safe where I was. However, as my career progressed and my leaders began to show that they understood my value, I persisted in upskilling myself and pushing for opportunities around the business that enabled me to exercise my neurodivergence and to thrive within the vast organism that is the brand. This eventually led me to my current innovation role, where I realized that my inner passion was to actually try to change the way the company did business and to help the people in the teams around the business get the most out of their jobs or to support innovations around customers getting the best experience or the most out of the company's products. It then gave me the scope to expand on my knowledge and to seek to find the unexpected insights, at this point feeding back to my internal and external stakeholders and develop new and diverse connections which encapsulated a diverse range of experiences and innovations in wider industries. And it was being given that freedom and support to cultivate my strength and attributes that led to my love for the business and my loyalty to their long-term goals and visions.'

It was a really interesting discussion because, although it's rare for companies to champion and support neurodivergent individuals, it's not unheard of, as I will explore in a moment. But for me it was refreshing to hear about his company's approach and support over the years and it gives me hope that some industries are turning a corner when it comes to building sustainable processes around their overarching wellbeing initiatives and staff development.

Before I closed the interview with Matt I wanted to see if he could give any advice to HR or people leaders who were looking to champion neurodiversity and innovate within their business and he told me this: 'Do not pay it lip service. Reasonable adjustments are only a first step and we must consider inclusive design in all aspects. This is not just about the Autism Act 2009 but about people, and we need to move away from this concept that everyone thinks like me, looks like me, acts like me. Especially when it comes to recruitment, as this homogeny does not reflect the community we work in or serve.'

Other examples of good practice

So, I mentioned that Matt's organization isn't the only company I found to be embracing the neurodiverse within its employee contingent. During my research I have come across several companies who have successfully harnessed neurodivergent thinking, demonstrating the positive impact it can have on innovation, creativity and workplace culture. So let them serve as a guiding light to others.

- **Microsoft:** Microsoft has been a pioneer in neurodiversity hiring initiatives all over the world. The company actively seeks neurodivergent talent through its Autism Hiring Program, recognizing the unique skills and perspectives that neurodivergent individuals bring to the technology industry. Through this programme, applicants engage in an extended interview process that focuses on workability, interview preparation and skill assessment. This process also gives candidates the opportunity to showcase their unique talents while learning about Microsoft as an employer of choice.[3]

- **SAP:** SAP, the multinational software corporation, has embraced neurodiversity in its workforce. The company's Autism at Work programme focuses on hiring individuals with autism and provides support structures to ensure their success within the organization.[4]

- **Ernst & Young (EY):** EY has implemented neurodiversity initiatives, including the Neurodiversity Centres of Excellence. These centres focus on hiring neurodivergent individuals and providing tailored support to help them thrive in their roles.[5]

- **Auticon:** Auticon is one of the world's leading employers of autistic adults in the technology sector. By recognizing the strengths of neurodivergent individuals, Auticon has created a business model that capitalizes on the unique skills and abilities of its employees. They even went as far as developing a free guide to help other companies who wish to learn from their experience and match their values.[6]

Conclusion

My fundamental conclusion here is that harnessing neurodivergent thinking has the potential to revolutionize both personal lives and businesses. By recognizing and celebrating the unique strengths and perspectives of neurodivergent individuals, we pave the way for increased innovation, creativity and inclusivity.

As individuals, embracing neurodiversity involves self-acceptance, advocacy and the pursuit of passions. For businesses, creating environments that prioritize diversity and inclusion through inclusive hiring practices, training initiatives and flexible work policies is clearly the key to sustainable success.

We can see from the success stories of companies like Microsoft, SAP, Ernst & Young and Auticon that it's a demonstrable fact that neurodiversity is not only beneficial for individuals but also contributes to the success and overarching resilience that underpins successful organizations and their evolution. So, as we collectively work towards a more inclusive future, the harnessing of neurodivergent thinking stands as a testament to the transformative power of diversity in shaping a world where every individual, regardless of their neurological or diverse makeup, can thrive and contribute in a meaningful and purposeful way.

Notes

1 Ironhack. Neurodiversity in tech: Embracing different perspectives for…, 13 January 2024. www.ironhack.com/gb/blog/neurodiversity-in-tech-embracing-different-perspectives-for-innovation (archived at https://perma.cc/LX4K-LTSS)

2 Wired Consulting. Why neurodiversity is a competitive advantage, 2024. www.wired.com/sponsored/story/why-neurodiversity-is-a-competitive-advantage-ey/ (archived at https://perma.cc/N9QT-NANS)

3 C Fang. Microsoft neurodiversity hiring program and FAQ, Microsoft, 2024. https://www.microsoft.com/en-us/diversity/inside-microsoft/cross-disability/neurodiversityhiring (archived at https://perma.cc/C4UK-RVHU)

4 SAP Careers. Embracing neurodiversity in the workplace, 2024. jobs.sap.com/content/Autism-at-Work/ (archived at https://perma.cc/DL26-MLS3)

5 Ernst and Young. Neurodiverse perspectives can help drive innovation, 2024. www.ey.com/en_ca/consulting/neurodiversity-centres-of-excellence-ey-canada (archived at https://perma.cc/HZS9-3GVQ)

6 Auticon. Auticon releases new guide to neurodiversity in the workplace, 11 May 2023. auticon.com/us/auticon-releases-neurodiversity-workplace-guide/ (archived at https://perma.cc/2SYH-2487)

5

The power of neurodiverse individuals and leaders

Neurodiverse leadership represents a paradigm shift in our understanding of leadership qualities and styles. You may have noticed that, as awareness of neurodiversity grows, organizations are increasingly recognizing the unique strengths that neurodivergent leaders and individuals bring to the table. So, I wanted to delve into the characteristics that often make neurodiverse leaders and individuals more effective, the advantages they bring to various roles, and how embracing neurodiversity in individuals and leaders contributes to organizational evolution and sustainability. The best way to begin is with a story of success.

INSIGHT: Starting with the individual

Lydia Stott is a Young Ambassador for the National Autistic Society, and while she is still in the early stages of her career, she has also accelerated within her company Cooper Parry (a Certified B Corp) to become a prominent Diversity and Inclusion Advisor to over 600 staff across the business.

Lydia was diagnosed with autism a month before she turned 18, so it's important to recognize that only in her adult life has she learnt to listen to and respect her needs as they differ from a neurotypical person's needs.

Working in HR as a Diversity and Inclusion Coordinator, Lydia absolutely loves her job, 'because it really ties into my strong sense of justice, my strategic and analytical way of thinking and my desire to support other neurodivergent and disabled people in the workplace. I was even recently highly commended by the Business Disability Forum for my work improving the accessibility of my workplace for neurodivergent employees.'

Lydia's first job was doing fairly basic data entry for a London start-up. 'I worked remotely because it enabled me to control my sensory environment. I never had to worry about the lighting, extra sounds or unexpected changes that I would've expected in an office. It also meant there was an extra barrier around unplanned social interaction. A lot of allistic people (people outside the autism spectrum) complain about feeling disconnected when working remotely, but it gave me a lot more confidence in my workplace relationships. Also, I wasn't expected to pick up on body language through a camera screen and always had a warning before I had to interact with someone, and I could feign internet issues if I needed to leave a social interaction due to anxiety.'

However, it was after only two months working full time in this job that Lydia realized, 'I was burning out a lot more than others doing the same job. This was because I was working in a system designed for neurotypical people and so I was having to work out my differences, things like light and noise sensitivity needs and necessary workplace adjustments that would make me more comfortable and less triggered during the working day, all while maintaining the same level of output as the rest of the team. I also find social interactions and the general sensory experience of being alive more tiring than many allistic people and so my energy levels were being entirely used up during the working day, leaving me nothing for recreational activities outside of work. And because I would work intensely, as I'm great at what I do, but more a sprinter not a marathon runner when it comes to work, I felt the need at this point to reduce my working to part-time, which had a hugely positive impact on my overall wellbeing.'

While learning more about how autism impacted her in the workplace, Lydia got the opportunity to join the Diversity and Inclusion Committee to lead a campaign for Neurodiversity Awareness Month and it was at this point she discovered her passion for diversity and inclusion, and it has gone on to become one of her favourite special interests. It was also a beautiful thing that her workplace recognized her passion and encouraged her to use it to benefit everyone in the company. And as a result of her campaign, she became aware of at least three people who realized they were neurodivergent and went on to get diagnoses.

Lydia's second job was working as an apprentice accountant, 'a great job for an autistic person as it requires a lot of attention to detail, routines and repetitive processes, as well as independent working. However, at this company in this specific team there was a significant lack of awareness about autism. This wasn't due to a lack of care or desire to learn, but because I was the first openly autistic person in the company the burden of education lay heavily with me. Again, this impacted my energy levels because I was having to teach everyone around me about my differences, or why I worked in a specific way and how they should lean into my strengths. During this time, there were attempts at accommodations, like a specialist work coach brought in to support me and my line manager working out adjustments, and I was allowed to work from home more often than other team members, while my manager tried to support me as best as she could within her own capacity and understanding.

'Ultimately, however, my director just didn't get it. I realized that their expectations were different: for them, accommodations were a temporary measure to get me working in the same way as everyone else, while for me, accommodations were a permanent system to allow me to work in my own way and continue to provide exceptional output for the company long-term, but I knew I would never be able to work in the same way as others.

'I just felt judged for not fitting in and was constantly tripped up by social subtext. For example, my director suggested a meeting time and asked, "Does that work for you?" and I told her it wasn't especially convenient – because I thought my director was *genuinely* asking if it worked for me. I would receive negative leadership commentary like "I say jump, you ask how high", which is clearly not the way to deal with anyone in your business, let alone a neuro-divergent team member.'

Now working as a Diversity and Inclusion Coordinator, Lydia gets to lean into her special interests. She gets to spend her time educating the company about different experiences and challenges faced by those in marginalized groups and tackling systemic barriers. This company clearly recognized it had a need and it also recognized Lydia's strengths, which means that Lydia now feels 'incredibly proud to work for a company that is so flexible and willing to adapt to improve the workplace experience for all employees equitably'.

Her favourite part of the job is that she gets to 'be the person that I needed when I was working as an apprentice accountant. I get to advocate for neurodivergent employees; while utilizing my time and energy to educate managers and teams which frees up the employees to concentrate on succeeding in their job; and I'm now learning how to be a coach to help disabled people work out the adjustments they need to thrive in the workplace.'

One initiative that Lydia is especially proud of is that her company will now fund a private diagnostic assessment for any employee who thinks they might be neurodivergent, which is inspiring. However, this should be a standard for every business. A big problem that we see is that 20 per cent of the population is neurodivergent and many go undiagnosed, and according to a global study by Alludo work-places are failing the neurodiverse demographic.[1]

With the above in mind, I was working for a client recently who had around 120 staff and they only had four people in the company who were officially recognized as neurodivergent. So based on what we know, there should be at least 20–24 staff who were neurodiverse in some way and there must be some that were undiagnosed. I then ran a coaching programme with six of their staff and found that four of these flagged as high propensity for ADHD when I ran some initial testing with them. This initiative shone a light on the issue, and I then advised that the company send out some links via their wellbeing channels that would allow staff to test themselves and see whether they might have neurodivergent indicators as a result of the initial tests and then set about arranging for consultants to come in and do official testing to cover autism, ADHD and dyslexia, so that staff with concerns could get official certified results, without having to wait for years in the NHS queue. This meant that the company in question could more rapidly encourage and offer support to those individuals.

A further study published in the *Harvard Business Review* suggests that unemployment rates run as high as 80 per cent for neurodiverse individuals. And companies like SAP have even re-designed their HR process to attract diverse talent. However, their Chief Diversity and Inclusion Officer states that if they were to use these same HR processes across all staff then they would miss out on attracting people with autism, for example, as the process just doesn't fit.[2]

It's important to understand that this job works for Lydia because it plays to her strengths and passions, but it also works because she now has a director who 'gets it'. Her line manager also sees and celebrates Lydia's strengths and focuses on output, not time or process, as well as actively educating herself about autism, so that she can best support Lydia, while being willing to be flexible, knowing that her role is to support Lydia to be the best she can be.

It's been a long journey for Lydia to get to this stage, because, in general, workplaces haven't been designed with autistic people in mind. So, it's important to consider some of the common difficulties an autistic person might face when starting in an office job.

So, how do you create a workplace that works for neurodiverse employees?

Lydia suggested the following:

- 'Autistic people often have different sensory needs that aren't met in offices. Lighting, sounds, temperature, screens, uniforms and dress codes can make an office uncomfortable for individuals like me. Being in an environment that I can't control for seven to nine hours a day can be a lot.'

- 'Social rules also differ in a professional environment, especially around hierarchy. One of the hardest challenges for me was working out what the differences were between the relationships with colleagues, managers and friends, because nobody ever explains this. An individual on the autism spectrum may also need to be conscious of how masking impacts their energy levels and work quality. If the individual is concentrating their efforts on fitting in and picking up on implicit communication, how can they expect themselves to be performing to the best of their ability? And that's before an employee like me even starts thinking about the expectations at lunch and work socials and if it's rude to point out when I see a process can be improved upon!'

- 'Those on the autism spectrum might also struggle with executive function, which is often not understood or treated with compassion by allistic people. If an office or work environment is new to them, systems they might have developed for themself in school or in home life might not be transferrable. Things like time management, project organization, task prioritization and coping with unexpected changes to their plans. If someone cancels a meeting at the last minute, I might lose about half an hour just processing the change.'

- 'Another very real challenge I have faced, as do many, is judgement and discrimination. There's a reason why only 22 per cent of autistic adults are in any kind of paid employment, and it's not because only a fifth of them are capable. Being different in a workplace can make you vulnerable, especially if your talents aren't recognized and your needs aren't respected, so it's totally reasonable for this fear to impact autistic people in the workplace.'

Lydia is someone who openly admits that, in many ways, she 'speaks from a position of privilege', and so she wanted to highlight to me that 'it's important to acknowledge that there is a multiplying effect on the barriers to work when you consider, in addition to any diagnosis, elements like class, race, further disabilities and other factors that may impede progression. When considering the challenges that autistic people face within the workplace, it's important to remember that within the autism spectrum there will be a vast difference in experiences and an individualized approach must always be taken.'

She continued, 'If you are an individual who struggles with sensory differences, acknowledge that and control your sensory environment to suit you. Wear headphones and earplugs, bring stim toys into meetings, wear clothes within the dress code that bring you comfort and confidence. Don't be afraid to meet your sensory needs in the office. I was always worried that I'd be judged when I came down to London to deliver training to fancy professionals in financial services about diversity and inclusion wearing funky dungarees and sunglasses in the office; however, having freedom of choice means that I run some really great training sessions, because when my needs are met I can do my best work.'

If, as an individual, you know organization is one of your challenges, try different strategies to suit you. Lydia would admit that 'none of what I suggest is especially groundbreaking, but sometimes you just need to give yourself permission to work in a different way to how everyone else seems to cope. Do you prefer to-do lists on a spreadsheet, in a notebook, using a task list app? Why not use your calendar to set yourself a hundred weekly reminders if you need to? Break down your regular processes into checklists or visual flowcharts for each step, then print this out and stick it on your desk. Figure out how your brain processes information and develop a system of organization that leans into that. For example, I will colour-coordinate all of my to-do lists, minutes, emails and produced work to make it very visual for me.

Depending on your job, what your workday looks like can vary immensely. Listen to your need for routines and make your working life work for you. Again, it's nothing revolutionary, but you're allowed to block time out for yourself at the start and end of each day to review your to-do list. You can have set times in your calendar for responding to emails, you can even set an autoreply to let people know what times you're likely to be responding. Remember to take breaks, especially if a stressful event happens like a last-minute change to a meeting time, and take care of yourself, because no allistic person is working flat-out 100 per cent of the time.'

If you're anything like Lydia, communication in the workplace might feel like a minefield to you. So here are a few techniques Lydia uses to support herself. 'In meetings, I always take minutes and send a summary email afterwards of key action points, which helps prevent misunderstandings around expectations and leaves a clear line of accountability. Know that workplace relationships are generally more formal than non-work friendships, even if a workplace refers to itself as a "family". For example, you can share what activities you did at the weekend, but you can't necessarily share anything intimate or emotional. Keep it to facts. Another thing I do is set myself on "Do not disturb" if I need focus time, a break from socializing or if I'm having a non-speaking period. And, finally, consider disclosing your autism. As I already mentioned, discrimination and judgement are very real, so it's okay if you don't feel comfortable sharing. But disclosure can help your managers or directors to learn how to support you and encourage your workplace to provide suitable accommodations that enable you to succeed.'

What can we as leaders do to address those challenges and help people thrive in the workplace? Lydia's first and most important tip is to 'recognize that anyone as an individual can contribute so much to the workplace. As an autistic person in a neurotypical world, it's easy to be made to feel less than. It's so important to establish that this is not true. Individuals on the autism spectrum should spend time working out what you do well, what your skills are, what kind of work you do best and why you are a brilliant employee to have, while companies should focus on supporting their neurodivergent employee's self-esteem, and where possible shape their work so you're playing to their strengths.'

When it comes down to what workplaces can offer, Lydia believes that one of the biggest challenges she found was 'knowing what adjustments I could ask for', so these are a few ideas of some requests you can make as an individual that might help you move forward:

- Flexible working arrangements can include reducing your hours, flexing when you work those hours, or being able to work from home some of the time. Office jobs generally have more opportunities for flexible working arrangements than industries like retail. Ask your manager if you can explore some different options to get the best out of you.

- One accommodation Lydia had was a mentor at work. This was a sort of buddy system where she was paired up with someone who was able to support her in the non-work elements of being in the workplace. Her mentor was around to answer questions and would also check in with Lydia semi-regularly. Lydia also most commonly forwarded her mentor messages from other colleagues, asking, 'Is this what this person really means or are they trying to say something else?' That mentor also helped Lydia to learn the unspoken rules of the office and helped proofread some of her emails for tone.

- More and more offices are incorporating sensory or wellbeing rooms. Sometimes they also function as prayer rooms. Ask about this in your office, and if there is one don't be afraid to use it. Lydia uses the wellbeing room in her office if she feels close to meltdown or sensory overload.

- Assistive technology is also constantly advancing. A government scheme in the UK called Access to Work means companies can even have assistive technology reimbursed. Things like adaptive keyboards or screens, a tablet for taking notes, noise-cancelling headphones or different computer programs can be helpful.

- And finally, your manager's role is to support you to be the best you can be at work. Support from your manager might look like weekly check-in meetings to review your to-do list, communicating explicitly with you about expectations and advocating for you to access these other accommodations, so engage with your manager and ensure you have that support.

When companies implement personal strategies and reasonable adjustments effectively, autistic people can be incredible additions to the workplace. Diversity in general brings innovation and new ideas and autistic people can bring fresh perspectives. Everyone in the world has different talents, but the shared traits of autistic people can often result in some specific strengths relevant to the workplace.

Attributes of neurodivergent leaders

While I've already mentioned some of the strengths that neurodivergent people often possess, and we can clearly see how Lydia has made herself a more effective individual, I think it's worth drawing on Lydia's insights and looking at how to understand these strengths better in the context of leadership.

We know already that neurodiversity refers to the natural variation in neurological traits present in the human population. We have also established that neurodivergent individuals often possess unique cognitive styles and perspectives. But the most important aspect surrounding these subtleties is recognizing and valuing these differences, while understanding that diverse ways of thinking contribute to innovative problem-solving, creativity and overall team effectiveness, which are inherent traits of any good leader, so neurodiverse leaders often exhibit a range of characteristics that contribute to their effectiveness in various leadership roles.

Neurodivergent leaders frequently bring innovative and unconventional approaches to problem-solving. Their ability to think outside traditional boundaries can lead to creative solutions and a fresh perspective on challenges. Many neurodivergent individuals excel in tasks requiring a high level of attention to detail. In leadership roles, this meticulousness can contribute to thorough planning, accurate decision-making and successful project execution. In addition, neurodivergent leaders often demonstrate the ability to hyper-focus on specific tasks or areas of interest. This intense concentration can lead to the development of specialized skills, making them valuable assets in areas that require deep expertise, but because neurodivergent leaders exhibit this deep passion and commitment to their areas of interest, this enthusiasm can inspire and motivate teams, fostering a positive and dedicated work environment. And most often these leaders may approach decision-making with a high degree of objectivity, focusing on facts and data rather than being swayed by emotional factors. This can result in well-considered and rational choices.

One of the most 'in demand' attributes among leaderships teams is resilience and navigating a world that may not always accommodate their differences. Neurodivergent individuals very often develop extreme resilience and adaptability. In leadership, this can translate to the ability to navigate change, overcome challenges and lead through uncertainty, which is something every leadership team is looking for in spades. A study by People Management suggested that only 29 per cent of staff across the UK and Europe feel they are resilient. A further aspect to that study suggested that, of those who felt they were not resilient, 59 per cent had lower engagement and were 43 per cent less likely to want to stay with their employer than those who felt resilient.[3]

But, for me, the thing that can really move your company needle is this. If neurodivergent individuals and leaders are given the flexibility and support to openly embrace their neurodiversity, then they organically create a culture of acceptance and inclusion. And this inclusive environment fosters higher levels of employee engagement, loyalty and overall job satisfaction, leading to higher productivity and reduced absenteeism.

So, if you embrace the diversity within your business and encourage those who are neurodivergent towards leadership roles, you are setting the company up for much wider success across the board.

Neurodiverse leaders often excel in recognizing and harnessing the strengths of their team members, and this talent-focused approach contributes to improved talent management, employee development and overall team performance, but in addition neurodivergent leaders tend to exhibit adaptive leadership styles, tailoring their approaches to the unique needs of their team members, as they recognize the needs they had to navigate during their own journey. This flexibility contributes to effective leadership in diverse and dynamic work environments, as highlighted by Dr Ann Gaceri Kaaria and Dr Grace Karamunta Karemu in their article 'Cultivating neurodiverse connections through competent leadership'.[4]

Let's now take a closer look at some neurodiverse individuals who have succeeded in leadership.

Dr Temple Grandin

Dr Temple Grandin, a prominent advocate for individuals with autism, has made a significant contribution to the field of animal science. As a neurodivergent leader, her unique perspective and innovative thinking

have revolutionized the treatment of animals in the agriculture industry. She states, 'Autism is part of who I am, it's not a tragedy and I
don't want to be cured. My brain is unique, and I wouldn't trade it for
anything.'

Steve Jobs

The late Steve Jobs, co-founder of Apple Inc, was known for his
intense focus, innovative thinking and attention to detail. While not
formally diagnosed, Jobs is believed by many to have had neurodivergent traits, contributing to his iconic leadership style and success
in the technology industry. Steve once quipped, 'Here's to the crazy
ones – the misfits, the rebels, the troublemakers, the round pegs in the
square holes. The ones who see things differently – they're not fond
of rules. You can quote them, disagree with them, glorify or vilify
them, but the only thing you can't do is ignore them because they
change things. They push the human race forward and while some
may see them as the crazy ones, we see genius, because the ones who
are crazy enough to think that they can change the world, are the
ones who do.'

Dame Stephanie Shirley

Dame Stephanie Shirley, a successful entrepreneur and philanthro-
pist, founded the software company Freelance Programmers. As a
neurodivergent leader, she has been a trailblazer in the technology
sector and a vocal advocate for diversity in the workplace. She
suggests, 'I've always been involved in research – first in computing,
later in autism. As a researcher, then a government adviser on research,
now a funder of medical research: helping to find what autism is, as
distinct from what it looks like. Research is slow and sometimes
produces absolutely nothing. But it's wonderful when you find yourself the first person to know something. Research is humbling. I am
lucky to still have things to get up for each morning. Much that other
people find important is just "stuff". I focus on ideas, on learning and

on innovation generally – the things that I know and care about. I work hard, recover from the many blind alleys and am motivated to succeed. My success was found at the edge of failure.'

INSIGHT: Inspired by Tourette's

When I was planning this chapter, I particularly wanted to interview Luke Manton, a successful young, gay entrepreneur. Luke had been told he was unemployable due to his Tourette's diagnosis and that he was only good for a life on benefits. So, he hired himself!

Since losing his job because of his perceived disability, where his superiors weren't willing to wait for a formal diagnosis and just saw his Tourette's as disruptive to the work environment, Luke has gone on to build his own successful virtual assistant agency and regularly supports individuals to find work through the 'access to work' scheme, while volunteering his services to create awareness and understanding for Tourette's charities and neurodivergent communities alike.

I originally met Luke at a TEDx event where he was speaking, and I was enraptured by his charismatic and comedic approach to sharing such a vulnerable story of success. I just had to know more.

Initially, my first focus when interviewing Luke was to understand what the perks were, because although we see analytical and creative observations with diagnoses like autism and ADHD, people tend to relate negative traits to those who manage Tourette's, so I wanted to gauge from him what traits that are clearly related to Tourette's have best served him in the context of his adaptability throughout his career to date.

Luke suggested to me, 'The traits I've picked up from living with Tourette's have really shaped how I operate and remain resilient in my career. Dealing with Tourette's means my life is all about adapting to changes, and this has been a game-changer at work. It's like I have got this built-in flexibility that helps me switch gears or tackle new projects without missing a beat. In today's fast-moving work world, being able to pivot on the fly is a superpower and it's one I believe I use to the max.

'Another aspect is the concept of facing the unexpected. With Tourette's, surprises are par for the course, so I can see that, over time, I have become pretty good at handling whatever work throws my way while maintaining a cool head. This knack for staying calm and collected when things get wild has been a huge asset for me, especially when it's crunch time or when plans go sideways.'

His day-to-day life is all about pushing through discomfort, which he suggests is like a daily drill, and that has translated into a killer work ethic and a stick-to-it attitude that keeps him grinding even when things get tough. 'It's all about keeping your eye on the prize, and my experience with Tourette's has taught me how to stay focused and motivated, no matter what.

'But in addition to this is my dedication. Living with Tourette's means I have had to double down on commitment, whether it's to manage symptoms or just get through the day. And this level of dedication spills over into my work, making me the kind of person who doesn't just meet expectations, I smash them.'

In essence, this means that, overall, Luke's understanding of his Tourette's has led to him lean into becoming 'organically more adaptable, cool under pressure, perseverant, dedicated, versatile, resilient and ready to take on whatever comes my way, and I would never change that!'

I was also interested to learn a bit more about Luke's thoughts around what concerns he thought companies were currently facing when cultivating neurodiverse individuals into leadership roles and how he would tackle those concerns as a successful business owner in his own right.

Luke believes, 'Companies trying to bring neurodiverse talent into leadership positions often hit a couple of speed bumps and a lot of it boils down to the big F: fear. There's this vibe that because someone's brain is wired differently, they might not fit the traditional leadership mould. A lot of these apprehensions come from a place of misunderstanding, or worse, stereotypes picked up from movies or popular media that paint a very one-dimensional picture of neurodiversity.'

Luke suggested, 'As someone who's navigated the business world with a neurodiverse mind, I think the golden ticket is education and genuine understanding, because, first off, companies need to get schooled on what neurodiversity actually means and not just about the challenges. It's about recognizing the unique strengths and perspectives neurodiverse individuals bring to the table. We're talking innovation, resilience, problem-solving skills and a whole lot of creativity. Education can help dismantle those fears and replace them with informed appreciation.'

Now, how about addressing those concerns head-on as a successful business owner? Here's Luke's game plan:

- **Lead with empathy and understanding:** Create an environment where everyone feels valued for their contributions, not judged for their differences. This means having open conversations, offering support where needed and celebrating the diverse ways of thinking within the team.

- **Tailor leadership development programmes:** Recognize that a one-size-fits-all approach doesn't cut it. Design leadership training that's flexible and accommodating, allowing neurodiverse individuals to develop their skills in a way that makes sense for them. This might include mentorship, tailored training sessions or even adjusting communication methods.

- **Promote a culture of inclusion:** This goes beyond just hiring neurodiverse individuals. It's about creating a workplace culture where everyone's voice is heard, and diverse perspectives are not only welcomed but are actively sought out. This involves training all staff on neurodiversity, challenging stereotypes and encouraging everyone to embrace different ways of thinking.

- **Highlight success stories:** Nothing combats fear like cold, hard proof. Showcase the achievements of neurodiverse individuals within your company and in the wider industry. This not only celebrates their success but also serves as a powerful testament to the value they bring.

- **Encourage open dialogue:** Make it easy for employees to talk about their experiences and needs without fear of judgement. This open line of communication can lead to better support systems and adjustments that enable neurodiverse individuals to thrive.

At the end of the day, it's about breaking down those barriers of fear and misunderstanding. By educating ourselves and our teams, embracing empathy and creating a genuinely inclusive culture, we can unleash the full potential of neurodiverse talent in leadership roles.

Are you sensing a trend as you consume each chapter? Perhaps hearing this sort of thing from all sides might move the needle?

With such an invasive disorder like Tourette's, I was interested to know how Luke manages overwhelm, to ensure he continues to perform effectively day-to-day and whether he has any habits that help to keep him effective.

What Luke told me was, 'Navigating the workday with something as unpredictable as Tourette's can definitely throw in some extra curveballs. It's like trying to juggle while riding a unicycle – challenging, but not impossible. I don't want to sugar-coat it; there are days when it feels like an uphill battle for me because the condition varies a lot, which means what works one day might not cut it the next, but here's the scoop on how I manage to keep the show going and stay productive.

'I have an amazing team around me. They've built this incredible culture where everyone's got each other's backs and they especially look out for me. It's like having a safety net; knowing they understand and support me makes a huge difference. It takes some of the pressure off, knowing I don't have to hide my struggles or pretend everything's fine when it's not.'

Breaks are Luke's best friend. He says, 'Never underestimate the power of stepping away for a few minutes. When things get overwhelming, I will give myself permission to take a breather. It's not slacking off; it's necessary to recharge and come back stronger. And, honestly, it helps to prevent a full-on overload, which would be way more disruptive in the long run.'

Music is another big thing for Luke. 'There's something about having my favourite tunes playing in the background that helps keep the overwhelm at bay. It's like the beats and melodies give my brain something else to focus on, which can sometimes make the tics less intense. Plus, it's a great way to boost my mood and energy levels.

'And then there's knowing when to call it a day. On the really tough days, when it feels like too much, I will give myself the OK to stop working. It's not quitting; it's recognizing that pushing through could do more harm than good. It took me a while to get comfortable with this because there's always that nagging feeling that I should be doing more, but I've learned that listening to my body and taking care of my wellbeing has to come first. Otherwise, I won't be good to anyone, least of all myself.'

Luke said that there's no magic formula or anything. 'It's more about being flexible and adapting to the day-to-day changes. Some days are better than others and that's okay. The key for me has been learning to work with my Tourette's, not against it. Sure, it throws some challenges my way, but it's also taught me a lot about resilience, patience and the importance of a supportive community.'

I think Tourette's is one of those diagnoses that companies don't really know what to do with. However, one thing that I thought might be helpful to individual readers was to understand what Luke would say if he met someone who was newly diagnosed as having Tourette's, or struggling with that period of diagnosis while the evidence was obvious, as he did, and what advice he would give them to help them embrace their neurodivergence.

His first comment was about 'finding your tribe and connecting'. Luke believes that if you 'connect with people who are walking the same path, it's a game-changer'.

Luke himself stumbled upon a group through the charity Tourettes Action, and they set up twice-weekly Zoom calls. He believes, 'Even to say those chats were a lifeline for me would be an understatement. It was more than just talking; it was finding a community that truly gets it, because Tourette's can feel like you're on an island, even in a crowded room. Your friends and family might offer support, saying they understand, but it's a whole different ballgame when you're sharing space (even virtually) with people who actually live it. They know the tics, the looks, the frustrations and the random moments of humour that come with Tourette's, so finding people who really understand what it's like can be the difference between struggling alone and feeling supported. It's about seeing your experiences reflected in others and realizing, hey, I'm not the only one. This sense of community can help you start to accept yourself, quirks and all. It's not about changing who you are; it's about embracing your neurodivergence and recognizing it as a part of your unique journey.'

And beyond just finding your community, Luke believes that it's paramount to 'be kind to yourself. The road to self-acceptance can be bumpy and it's okay to have days where you're not feeling 100 per cent on board with this whole Tourette's thing. You should give yourself the grace to feel whatever comes up, knowing that it's all part of the process. And along the way, get curious about your Tourette's. The more you understand it, the better equipped you'll be to navigate the world with it. Knowledge is power and in this case it's also comfort.'

Luke also recommended, 'Don't hesitate to reach out for help when you need it. Whether it's professional support, joining support groups, or just having a chat with someone who gets it, remember that asking for help is a sign of strength, not weakness. And this goes for any neurodiversity.'

All of this individual growth is really important, but it seems that very often it's consistently on us as individuals to deal with our challenges and that companies aren't really getting to grips with neurodiversity or even managing diversity, equity or inclusion very well at all. So, my final conversation with Luke focused on the most important things that a company should consider when developing neurodivergent leadership teams and individuals, and how he felt companies should tackle those who might be challenged by their Tourette's in a more traditional working environment.

In a typically structured and engaging fashion, Luke offered five points:

- **Embrace the human touch:** First and foremost, remember we're all humans here. Treating everyone with respect, understanding and genuine care is key. For individuals with Tourette's or any neurodivergence, this human-first approach is especially crucial. It's not just about accommodations or adjustments; it's about recognizing each person's unique value and ensuring they feel seen and supported.

- **Open communication is everything:** This is so important – talk to your people! Open, honest communication is the cornerstone of any successful relationship and it's no different in the workplace. For those with Tourette's, having the space to express their needs, concerns and what works for them is vital. It's about creating a dialogue, not a monologue. Ask how you can support them, check in to make sure they're comfortable and truly listen to what they have to say.

- **Recognize limits and work within them:** Everyone has their limits, and for neurodiverse folks these boundaries might be different from what you'd expect. It's crucial for companies to understand and respect these limits. This means not pushing for change or overwhelm beyond what's manageable. It's about pacing things in a way that allows everyone to stay productive without burning out. Remember, productivity doesn't have to mean working at breakneck speed. It's about sustainable, effective work that takes everyone's capabilities into account.

- **Tailor support and accommodations:** Cookie-cutter solutions don't cut it when it comes to supporting neurodiverse teams. What works for one person might not work for another, especially for someone with Tourette's. Companies should be ready to tailor support and accommodations to fit the individual. This could mean flexible working hours, providing a quiet space for work, or allowing breaks when needed. It's about adapting the work environment to fit the person, not the other way around.

- **Foster an inclusive culture:** Building an inclusive culture is non-negotiable. This means going beyond just hiring neurodiverse individuals; it's about creating an environment where everyone feels they belong and can thrive. Celebrate diversity, provide training on neurodiversity to all staff and actively work to dismantle any stigma or stereotypes that might exist. An inclusive culture is one where differences are not just tolerated but valued and seen as strengths.

And when it comes to companies tackling support systems for those challenged by their Tourette's in a traditional working environment, Luke said, 'It boils down to treating them as individuals, with their own sets of strengths and needs. It's about creating a supportive, flexible and inclusive workplace where open communication and human-centric approaches are the norms. By focusing on these key areas, companies can ensure that their neurodiverse leadership teams and individuals are not just included but empowered to shine.'

Embracing neurodiverse leadership

So, lets recap some of what we learned in this chapter and through Lydia and Luke's journeys.

Key strategies for organizations

What should companies consider implementing when it comes to practical strategies for embracing neurodiverse leadership?

It may seem a little repetitive, but it's fundamental and it's not getting done, so until companies learn, us neurodivergent individuals will just keep trying to hammer it home!

- **Promote inclusive hiring practices:** Actively seek neurodivergent candidates during the recruitment process. Implementing inclusive hiring practices, such as alternative interview formats and accessible application processes, ensures a diverse pool of applicants.

- **Provide neurodiversity training:** Conduct training programmes for leadership teams to increase awareness and understanding of neurodiversity. These programmes can dispel myths, reduce stigma and promote a culture that values diverse cognitive styles.

- **Create accommodating work environments:** Design work environments that accommodate the diverse needs of neurodivergent leaders and team members. This may include providing sensory-friendly spaces, flexible work arrangements and access to assistive technologies.

- **Offer professional development opportunities:** Tailor professional development programmes to be accessible and inclusive. Recognize and support the unique learning styles of neurodivergent leaders, ensuring they have opportunities for continuous growth and skill development.

- **Establish neurodiversity employee resource groups (ERGs):** Forming neurodiversity ERGs within the organization creates a platform for networking, mentorship and shared experiences. These groups contribute to a sense of community and provide valuable insights for leadership teams.

- **Encourage open communication:** Foster a culture of open communication where neurodivergent leaders feel comfortable discussing their needs and preferences. Encourage all team members to express themselves and contribute their unique perspectives.

- **Provide mentorship and support:** Implement mentorship programmes that pair neurodivergent leaders with mentors who can provide guidance and support. Mentors can help neurodivergent leaders navigate challenges and develop their leadership skills.

- **Measure and celebrate success:** Establish metrics to measure the success of neurodiversity initiatives within the organization. Celebrate achievements, share success stories and highlight the positive impact of neurodivergent leadership on team dynamics and organizational outcomes.

Key challenges for individuals

While neurodiverse leaders bring valuable strengths to the table, it's essential to acknowledge and address the challenges they may face in leadership roles, so when defining how you champion neurodivergent staff or leaders within your business you should always keep in the back of your mind the three primary challenges:

- **Social communication challenges:** Neurodivergent leaders may experience challenges in social communication. Implementing communication strategies, such as clear and direct communication channels, can help bridge potential gaps.

- **Navigating organizational politics:** Neurodivergent leaders may encounter challenges in navigating organizational politics and interpersonal dynamics. Providing mentorship and support, along with transparent communication, can help them navigate these complexities.

- **Access to leadership opportunities:** Barriers to accessing leadership opportunities may exist for neurodivergent individuals. Organizations must actively promote inclusive leadership pathways and ensure equal opportunities for career advancement.

Conclusion

Neurodiverse leadership has the potential to redefine our understanding of effective leadership across the board. By recognizing and valuing the unique strengths that neurodivergent individuals bring to leadership roles, organizations can foster environments that promote innovation, inclusivity and success. Neurodivergent leaders, with their innovative thinking, attention to detail and resilience, contribute to enhanced problem-solving, employee engagement and overall organizational effectiveness, which will no doubt have an effect on uplifting the bottom line and making companies wholly more successful in the traditional sense, via untraditional methodology.

I generally find with my clients, and through the experience of people I interviewed as part of this book, that as businesses and leaders embrace the principles of neurodiversity, they not only unlock the potential of neurodivergent individuals but also contribute to a more inclusive and dynamic workplace culture. The case studies of leaders like Dr Temple Grandin, Steve Jobs and Dame Stephanie Shirley serve as inspiring examples of how neurodivergent thinking can lead to transformative impacts in various fields, but it is only by implementing practical strategies, overcoming barriers and celebrating success that organizations can harness the power of neurodiverse leadership to drive positive change and innovation in the evolving landscape of leadership and business globally.

Notes

1 Alludo. Global survey: The workplace is failing a major demographic, nd. www.alludo.com/en/newsroom/news/data-insights/neurodiversity-at-work-report/ (archived at https://perma.cc/G3LU-H6ZJ)

2 R D Austin and G P Pisano. Neurodiversity as a competitive advantage: Why you should embrace it in your workforce, *Harvard Business Review*, May/June 2017. hbr.org/2017/05/neurodiversity-as-a-competitive-advantage (archived at https://perma.cc/M4Y5-L483)

3 E Howlett. Only a third of UK employees feel resilient, survey finds, *People Management*, 9 September 2020. www.peoplemanagement.co.uk/article/1742912/only-a-third-of-uk-employees-feel-resilient (archived at https://perma.cc/P24W-NEF6)

4 A Gaceri Kaaria and G Karamunta Karemu. Cultivating neurodiverse connections through competent leadership: Integrative literature review, *International Journal of Advanced Research*, March 2024. www.researchgate.net/publication/378887233_Cultivating_Neurodiverse_Connections_Through_Competent_Leadership_Integrative_Literature_Review (archived at https://perma.cc/RL2B-X2HT)

6

Creating an inclusive culture

Diversity, equity and inclusion (DEI) are fundamental components of a thriving and sustainable business model. This inclusivity promotes employee morale, satisfaction and engagement, resulting in higher productivity and innovation, but moreover an inclusive workplace culture is one where every employee feels valued, respected and supported regardless of their background, identity or differences. It goes beyond mere tolerance to actively embracing diversity and creating an environment where everyone can bring their authentic selves to work. The essence of inclusivity lies in ensuring that every individual, regardless of their race, gender, sexual orientation, disability or any other characteristic, has equal opportunities, access to resources and a sense of belonging within the organization.

Studies by McKinsey between 2015 and 2020 suggest a strong business case for the evolution of DEI initiatives surrounding gender, ethnic and cultural diversity in leadership. These proactive studies have actually shown that companies that are more diverse outperform those that lack diversity or strong DEI strategies, and that the more diverse companies are infinitely more profitable, meaning that they will consistently outperform their competitive peers who are less focused on a diverse approach to diverse leadership structures.

When McKinsey did their 2019 analysis in advance of releasing their 2020 study, they found that companies who were in the upper quartile when it came to gender diversity within their executive teams were actually 25 per cent more likely to have a profitability that was above average, over companies in the lower quartile. In addition, this was an increase because in 2017 when they conducted the same study companies in the upper quartile were at 21 per cent more profitable and in their 2014 study there was only 15 per cent difference, so there's definitely been an incremental rise in profitability for these companies as they adopt, adapt and develop their teams with diversity in mind.

Another interesting finding was that the companies with more than 30 per cent of their executives being female were more likely outperform those companies who had a lower percentage of female executives.

Then when McKinsey delved further into ethnic and cultural diversity throughout 2019 the companies in that upper quartile were found to have outperformed the companies in the lower quartile by as much as 36 per cent when it came to profitability. This suggests strongly that there's actually a higher level of profitability when your company focuses more heavily on diversity in ethnicity over simply looking at gender balance.[1]

A 12-step DEI plan

With the above in mind, creating a diversity, equity and inclusion plan/policy, is crucial for fostering an inclusive workplace environment and for the impact it will inevitably have when lifting the bottom line, so I wanted to kick off this chapter with my personal 12-step DEI policy process to help those who might need support or guidance to set up an effective DEI strategy for your business. These are the fundamentals you should measure against. They may not all be relevant to everyone, but when you set about either building or reviewing an DEI strategy you should check against these 12 points, as it will either give you a foundation for what you need to achieve or help you to understand whether your current plan is covering the right bases.

1 **Assess your current state:** It's important for companies to conduct a thorough assessment of your overarching diversity landscape, including demographics surrounding your employees, but also

with a strong focus on your company policies, practices and inclusive culture. Ensure that you look to gather data on employee demographics, such as your staff retention rates and promotion rates, and measure any existing DEI initiatives for effectiveness based on the results you see off the back of actions taken.

2 **Establish clear objectives:** When balancing objectives and deliverables, you must also define specific, measurable, achievable, relevant and time-bound (SMART) goals for your DEI plan. There's no point in executing strategy without key performance indicators and a structured timeline for delivery and execution. As business leaders, you must ensure that you determine what you want to achieve in terms of diversity, equity and inclusion within your organization and then make employees aware of your values and tangible suggested measures to achieve results when working towards achieving those values when it comes to culture.

3 **Create a DEI task force:** As a company or a value-driven leader, form a diverse task force comprised of employees from different levels, departments and backgrounds to spearhead the development and implementation of the DEI plan. This will galvanize hearts and minds across the board, and you will have much more effective results and deliverables off the back of your initiatives. However, it's paramount to ensure that the task force represents the diversity of your workforce so that the dynamics are most effective, and each diverse group is championed as you define strategy and implement change.

4 **Educate and train your leaders and teams:** Many companies forget that this is an important step when developing an effective cultural strategy, but when you provide comprehensive training surrounding DEI for all employees, including leadership, you are effectively evolving the foundations of the culture that you want to create. And don't stop after the first round of training – it's imperative that you constantly and consistently implement new training measures and ideas along the way so that your employees and your company can adapt and evolve with the right knowledge that links back to your core values, business drivers and cultural

ambitions. You should be offering things like workshops, seminars, keynote speaker sessions/fireside chats and accessible resources to raise awareness, build empathy and enhance cultural competency throughout the organization. It's important to engage regularly with leaders and teams to let them know what's expected and what resources and support are available to them, to enhance competency, and moral and operational effectiveness.

5   **Regularly review policies and procedures:** Most companies that I meet do *not* do this! However, if the foundations are already there, then it's paramount to review existing policies, procedures and practices to identify any biases or barriers that may hinder equity and inclusion. Go back to your task force leaders and get feedback – find out what's working and what's being missed. Companies as well as individual leaders should be introspective in terms of understanding the needs of the wider organization. And once you've done those reviews, make a point of implementing any necessary provisions or amends to policies, to promote fairness and eliminate discrimination across areas like recruitment, hiring practices, issuance of promotions and decision-making processes.

6   **Specifically implement diversity-backed recruiting strategies:** Surprisingly few businesses actually have specific strategies in place. Instead, they simply gesture that they are open to all. But if you develop proactive strategies to attract and retain a diverse workforce then you will be the stronger for it, as we saw from the McKinsey study. You can even partner with diverse recruitment agencies and attend job fairs where you can specifically target underrepresented groups. Also, be sure to revise job descriptions to remove any biased language.

7   **Foster inclusive leadership:** Make a conscious decision to promote inclusive leadership behaviours among managers and executives, because this sets the tone for the whole organization, and you need to lead from the top down if you are to be effective. In addition to the training and education I mentioned in point number 4, you could also provide training and support to help leaders effectively manage diverse teams, so that they better understand how to address unconscious biases and create an inclusive workplace environment.

8 **Establish employee resource groups:** One of the most cost-effective ways to promote and establish cultural- and value-led change is to encourage the formation of ERGs or affinity groups that provide a supportive space for employees from marginalized or underrepresented communities to come together and discuss their needs. ERGs are not only effective when looking to understand the needs of individual communities, they can also operate as company think tanks where you can look for innovation that could impact the wider company business drivers. In addition, it's more cost effective than hiring a bunch of consultants to tell you how to evolve because it's backed by your people volunteering to be involved to help you shape their and the company's future. But be sure to allocate resources. That might include some budgets and support for ERGs to organize events, initiatives and advocacy efforts so that staff feel empower to innovate and implement change initiatives.

9 **Be dynamic and promote equity through compensation and benefits:** If you conduct regular pay equity audits to ensure fairness and transparency in compensation practices, then again you strive to improve moral and incentivize longevity and staff retention. For a start, review the wider employee benefits and ensure they meet the diverse needs of your workforce, then make changes and acknowledge what needs to be done long term to encourage regular assessments so employees have something to work towards. This will increase productivity in addition to retention and staff loyalty.

10 **Strive to create a culture of inclusion:** Every company and their respective business leaders should be aiming to foster a culture where all employees feel valued, respected and empowered to contribute their unique perspectives towards the betterment and evolution of the organization and their peers. If you also recognize and celebrate diversity through events, awards and initiatives like recognition programmes, then you will underpin the mindset that you care and that you are invested in cultural change at the core of what you do.

11 **Regularly measure progress and accountability:** Establish key performance indicators (KPIs) and metrics to track progress towards your DEI goals, just as you would across the business, whether it be in a sales function, or marketing for example. In addition, you should monitor and evaluate initiatives on a regular basis, collect anonymous feedback from employees and hold leaders accountable for advancing equity and inclusion. If you do this, they you will have the ability as a leader or as an organization to adapt and shift momentum and support to areas where it's most needed, as the companies and the employees needs change and evolve over time.

12 **Always focus on continuous improvement and adaptation:** DEI work is ongoing and requires continuous improvement and adaptation. Your leaders, your ESGs and your task force need to stay informed about emerging local and global best practices, investing time in research and fostering initiatives surrounding trends in diversity, equity and inclusion where you see things working for others. If you also regularly review and update your DEI plan to address evolving challenges and opportunities, as with any other aspect of the points I've mentioned above, then you will see sustainable and measurable change for the long term.

By following these 12 steps, you can create a robust diversity, equity and inclusion plan that fosters a more inclusive and equitable workplace for all employees, but the above is by no means all-encompassing, so take this as a structure and innovate for yourself as you develop each aspect. Don't be afraid to push boundaries and consider what your company and its employees might need in respect of your industry or how you operate as a business.

INSIGHT: Key elements of an effective strategy

Dr Shola Mos-Shogbamimu is a prominent BBC and ITV news correspondent, lawyer and activist, campaigning heavily for women's rights and the cultivation of diverse leaders in business. We've been friends since the early days of my career in wellbeing when we used to run the Institute of Directors' diversity and inclusion events around the country, before DEI was something businesses started taking more seriously. For this book, our discussion focused on where companies are currently most lacking when it comes to creating an inclusive workplace culture and strategies to overcome this.

Ultimately, Shola protests that she didn't 'see a tangible, sustainable movement of the dial in the last 10 years and in fact it started to look as though companies were getting it at one point several years ago and that people were starting to understand that diversity, equity and inclusion is, at the very least, integral to their bank balance, but realistically it's lost momentum and everyone seems to be flailing.'

Shola wanted me to consider that we need to 'wake up as a society and be less divisive' in how we perceive and operate in the world. She mentioned that her mantra is 'there are people who've gone before you and who've gone through these things, people whose shoulders we stand on, who've been abused, who've been discriminated against for whatever reason, and we are not new in our activism for change.' She said, 'Don't get me wrong, it's not a nice experience. I mean, you know, I've been getting death threats from extremists and the like, that's not a nice experience at all. But I trust I will be safe, and I continue to do what I am required to do, because the reason for the threats and the abuse is to silence our voices and to make us so afraid, or so embarrassed, or so humiliated, or so worried that I had better not say anything. But absolutely not! Your voice, even if initially it is a lone voice, must be heard and must be added to many others, in order to create the storm that will squash the injustice that we all see.'

So, with Shola's strength reverberating in my mind, I wanted to throw in some of the other elements that are imperative when you start trying to define and establish what you want your strategy to include when looking at workplace culture. You may see aspects of these crop up in different chapters, however it's important to recognize that each of these subheadings are seeds for strategies worth exploring in the wider context of DEI and not solely for use when looking at one specific area like neurodiversity. Many strategies apply to different decision-maker processes with varying specificities or contexts. What is important to remember with any educational tool is that you take what is valuable and shed what you don't need. And this book is no different! Here are the key elements for any effective strategy:

Leadership commitment and accountability

Inclusivity has to start at the top of the food chain. The companies whose senior leaders aren't coming forward to support wellbeing, culture and diversity are not getting traction. So, these senior leaders must demonstrate a genuine commitment to fostering an inclusive culture. This involves setting clear expectations, holding themselves accountable for progress and actively participating in initiatives that promote diversity and inclusion.

Shola told me, 'It's obvious that companies lack the will when it comes to leadership commitment and accountability. I believe that they do the bare minimum, and that bare minimum is usually to have policies that are compliant with applicable laws and regulations. Then they try to follow whatever the trend is at any given time. So, whatever is "hashtag" trending. The approach is very much "Let's quickly do that", or "Let's get that speaker in on this issue." But what these leaders are lacking is the fact that there is no root to their perceived commitment. There is no root in whatever policies or commitments they claim they have, so it's like trying to grow a tree without roots. The tree would never have grown in the first place. And that is why, on the issue of inclusion, companies today are still lacking so horribly. The point where inclusion differs from diversity is that inclusion is the execution of diversity. Diversity starts off with: we need a talent pool. OK, so let's go out there. Let's embrace people who are different. People who are human. They shouldn't have to fit whatever it is that companies consider "the norm". If you commit to making sustainable and tangible changes then you need to drive execution from the top down.'

Shola states that the norm is 'whatever we all are. Companies are generally clearly struggling with inclusion and can't demonstrate that their workforces have the feeling of being included, and that will always track back to this lack of commitment. My gut instinct is that if you took 100 companies tomorrow and tried to test their policies around inclusion, you would find that the policy doesn't match the reality of the lived experiences of their workforce. So, ultimately, those 100 companies have nothing more than nice words on a piece of paper, probably drafted by lawyers like me, but it means absolutely nothing in reality.'

This also rings true to my experience in business over two decades and my knowledge of the wellbeing space over the last 10 years, since before wellbeing and inclusion was 'PR popular'. I simply don't see enough senior leaders coming forward and representing the true needs of their wider populace and ultimately that's the problem – there's too much lip service, and not enough leaders are proactive in their commitment to change because no one wants to be accountable. There are already tools out there that will define where your business is bleeding money because of unhappy and disenfranchised staff, or mismanaged people and processes, but any CEO who shines a light on this will then be under pressure to make tangible and sustainable changes fast, to plug these holes, and if they don't they will lose the support of the board or shareholders and they will lose their job, so no one wants to do that.

Diversity training and education

Companies should implement regular diversity and inclusion training programmes, to help raise awareness and educate employees about the importance of inclusivity as a mindset, and work towards using this education to create a fundamental cultural shift throughout their organizations. These programmes can include focus areas like unconscious bias, micro-aggression and cultural competence, which in turn will support in fostering a more informed and empathetic workforce.

Equitable policies and practices

As I mentioned at the start of the chapter, companies must review and update policies and practices to ensure they are equitable and unbiased.

This includes recruitment and hiring processes, which are often missed, performance evaluations and promotions, alongside any other areas where biases may inadvertently influence decision-making.

When I interviewed Shola, I asked her whether she felt there is a correlation between cultivating diverse teams across our businesses and the subsequent success or failure of those businesses. Because people want to see the return on investment but are fearful of putting money into things like evolving hiring practices.

She said, 'One of the key things that many businesses have an issue with is their high staff turnover. And one of the key reasons I believe that people leave and actually plan an exit strategy is because they see no growth and no place for them in that organization. This stems from environments that are simply not equitable in the contexts of their policies and practices, so they just go. The mindset is very often that they've done their one year here, or their two years there, and they take what they need and they just leave. That is a direct correlation with the fact that an organization lacks an inclusive or effective diversity, equity and inclusive policy; not just a policy, but the reality of the environment that they have and the workplace culture are simply not there.'

Shola also mentioned the big issues surrounding the gender and ethnicity pay gap. We both agreed during the interview that we really couldn't understand why we're still talking about this in 2024. Shola suggested, 'There is very demonstrable evidence of companies lacking the will to evolve their policies and then relate that to sustainable best practices across the board, but it should not be difficult to deliver equity on pay. Fact! Another reason people pack up their bags and they leave. They put the smile on their face, do their jobs and they just leave on their own terms and leverage what they can, to the detriment of the business who should have looked after them in the first place.'

Employee resource groups

Establishing and supporting ERGs provides a platform for employees to connect, share experiences and advocate for inclusivity. These groups, focused on various aspects of diversity (e.g. race, gender, LGBTQ+), contribute to a sense of community within the organization.

The cornerstone, as Shola sees it, would consist of 'getting the buy-in of your workforce initially, so the people who stand to benefit are there and they are rallied. I also believe that every company should have people at a junior level or mid-level management sitting on the executive board, and that those people should represent the voices of the wider staff population. The best asset at a company is your staff, and if you do not have the buy-in of your staff you're really not going anywhere. Not as fast as you want to, anyway, and you could do a whole lot more, achieve a whole lot more if you have your staff invested in your company. So, getting the buy-in of your staff when it comes to decisions surrounding the workforce culture is paramount.'

Flexible work arrangements

It's now a prevalent opinion that offering flexible work arrangements can better accommodate the diverse needs of employees, whether that be someone with autism or ADHD who may suffer from sensory overload if they're in an office full time, or a new mother trying to balance their baby's early-stage care with maintaining a career, for example. This flexible approach could include options such as remote work, flexible hours and compressed workweeks, which should ulti-mately lead toward enabling individuals to balance their personal and professional responsibilities.

A whitepaper from Robert Walters, a recruitment group in South Africa, reviewed the impact of workplace flexibility on productivity, engagement and diversity. What they mentioned in this study is that employees tend to agree, or even strongly agree, with the concept that flexible working will help them to become more effective and in turn yield better results for the overarching business:

- 83 per cent said that they have achieved a higher level of motivation, with 80 per cent stating that the flexibility has given them an increased level of work–life balance.

- 70 per cent believe they are more focused and more productive as a result of flexible working and 69 per cent are of the opinion that, when implementing flexible working, they as individuals have a higher level of quality output in their work.

- When considering what sort of barriers companies might face getting leadership buy-in with regards to flexible working, 60 per cent agreed that the biggest concerns were related to the possibility of employees abusing the policy and taking advantage of the organization.[2]

Mentorship and sponsorship programmes

Another under-utilized concept that works well is to implement mentorship and sponsorship programmes that connect employees with mentors who can provide guidance and support. Very often, taking senior leaders within an organization and having them mentor staff voluntarily is the most effective way to do this. Sponsorship also involves advocating for employees' career advancement and ensuring they have equal opportunities for growth.

Transparent communication

Foster open and transparent communication about the organization's commitment to inclusivity. This could be through a regular newsletter, awareness events or engaging senior leaders to speak openly about future company changes when it comes to culture- or value-driven change. Clearly communicate goals, progress and any changes related to diversity and inclusion initiatives with staff, because this is also reinforcing the organization's values and transparency and further fosters trust and loyalty.

Inclusive language and communication

Always pay attention to language and communication to ensure it is inclusive and respectful, especially throughout company communications, directives, white papers and such, which cover DEI specific topics. Avoiding gendered language, using inclusive pronouns and being mindful of cultural sensitivities contribute to a more welcoming and inclusive environment and again this will increase employees' desire to adopt change.

Celebrating diversity

Many larger organizations actively celebrate cultural and religious holidays, awareness months and other significant events, because this not only acknowledges the diversity within the organization but also educates employees about different cultures and perspectives. And these initiatives should always be open to all staff, which helps to foster connection and allyship.

The problem, as Shola sees it, is that 'companies still need it to be sold to them, making them understand that, by diversifying their pool of talent, more women, more people from different backgrounds, with neurodivergent traits, what you're actually doing is celebrating diversity and creating a workplace culture that organically gets richer and richer, and this will inevitably feed into the quality of work. It will also feed into the quality of the environment people are in and help people to thrive, in turn helping your company thrive, but I don't think companies are getting that. Look at what Elon Musk said, in the context that he's probably the richest man on Earth apparently and chanting about the concept DEI (diversity, equity and inclusion) must DIE. That is not progress, my brother, that is not progress! If we don't celebrate our differences as human beings, then we are simply not evolving as a species.'

Shola went on to comment, 'The dominant men, mainly dominant white men, they stop pushing black people forward, they stop pushing women forward, they stop pushing people forward who are different, trying to show that these people can't handle the stress, they can't handle the pressure and so why are they in the workplace? Ultimately it just shows that we are not celebrating diversity or human individuality enough and we are regressing not progressing across the board, hence all the lip service and reactive wellbeing and inclusion schemes over anything proactive or progressive. We must start celebrating diversity and mean it!'

Feedback mechanisms

It is vital to establish mechanisms for employees to provide feedback on inclusivity efforts. This can include surveys, focus groups or confidential channels for reporting concerns. Because we don't evolve if we don't learn, and unless we risk failing, or seeing where we are failing, then we are never going to evolve. Most importantly, companies and leaders need to be open to both the positive and negative feedback and not shy away from asking questions to avoid the negative. You also need to act on feedback to continually improve and refine inclusivity initiatives, because being proactive is going to improve the culture and the effectiveness of the individuals and the organization.

In addition, companies need to really start to test their DEI policies against real incidents. Shola believes that 'companies should be back taking a look at previous incidents that were flagged in relation to diversity and inclusion to see how they dealt with those issues and whether it actually matches up with the reality of what they think they have in place to safeguard employees. Because only in genuinely testing policies and process do you fully understand if you've got a robust strategy or a weak link in the fence.'

Accessibility and accommodations

It is another fundamental consideration to ensure that physical and digital spaces are accessible to individuals with varying disabilities. Implement accommodations as needed, depending on the make-up of your workforce. Providing assistive technologies, accessible facilities and accommodations for neurodivergent individuals is a good starting point from which to build.

Promoting intersectionality

Recognize and address the intersectionality of identity. Inclusivity efforts should consider the unique experiences and challenges faced by individuals who belong to multiple marginalized groups, as you saw from the experience detailed in my interviews with leaders like Dr Samantha Hiew and Lee Chambers, fostering an environment that acknowledges and supports their diverse needs.

Addressing unconscious bias

Implement programmes specifically designed to address unconscious bias within the workplace. This may involve unconscious bias training, workshops and ongoing education to help employees recognize and mitigate biases in their decision-making.

And for the individuals reading this thinking 'That's easier said than done', or feeling underrepresented, I wanted to delve a little bit into Shola's career, because throughout she's suffered from significant prejudice, some of which has been very extreme and must have been emotionally challenging. Race hate crimes and all sorts have been prevalent for her because of the nature of her wanting to change the state of play societally.

I asked Shola how she, as an individual, has managed to maintain such a positive, focused and dynamic mindset to become so successful in terms of what she does. She told me, 'In reality, my faith is what keeps me strong to some degree. Moreover, my relationship with God. And, to be honest, I don't do religion and religion is not me, but I do have a personal relationship with what I term "God", which is much more spiritual. When people attack me, I would say that it's generally because they don't like the truth – the truth is controversial, not gentle. And because I am the vessel with which this truth is coming out, they attack me. But I have no problem with talking about issues or injustices as I find them, and I have no qualms whatsoever about putting people in their place when necessary.'

Shola would suggest that 'most people that take issue with me think the best way to deal with this "black woman" is to put me down. They can't debate me on an issue, so they want to discredit me. And where I believe my faith comes into the mix is when I am able to remember who I am and what is good inside me.'

If companies can support the understanding of unconscious bias and celebrate their cultural diversity within the business, then perhaps more people will feel valued and heard and won't have to endure what Shola has, which has ultimately come off the back of an ignorant mindset and approach to leadership control.

Creating allies and advocates

It's always important not to specifically segregate minority groups, even when you develop initiatives like ERGs, because you need to encourage the development of allies and advocates for inclusivity within the organization. Allies will actively support and promote inclusivity, while advocates take a more proactive role in driving systemic change. As a company you should be encouraging the engagement of individuals who want to learn to become allies and advocates, as you develop initiatives for change.

Shola told me that she thinks as individuals 'we need to be a reflection of what we believe', so, for instance, 'me being part of a small process of your book, is about me lending my voice, my love, my joy in your accomplishments, and that can be reflected in how other people can see. So, while we two people have totally different backgrounds, people will see that we get along and we have a friendship where there is mutual respect.' Shola went on to say that she believes that 'the best thing that anyone can do is just to go about living your life in the way you believe you should live it and let that be the evidence of who you are.' Shola told me that 'for you and I Thomas our lives should be a mirror of what we actually believe and we don't need to go out and say to people who we are or what our relationship is, because they will see it, they will see the engagement. They'll see how we get on; they will see it when they happen to see us on the street or see us at an event or read your book. And that's what I believe is the best way we can help shape society and also to share our learning with the next generation.'

Remember, when you review the points in this chapter, that my first 12 steps are what an DEI policy should fundamentally include, and these follow up sub-sections are an example of the various strategies that you could implement that relate to those 12 steps. This breakdown should give you a steer on how to select a strategy topic that you can build on.

INSIGHT: The challenges of building an inclusive culture

To gain ready insights in this area, I interviewed an inspiring man called Silvan Ruthenberg. Silvan has both an autism and ADHD diagnosis and used to put his neurodiversity to good use as a Senior Account Director at LinkedIn, but is now more notably known through his role as the Global Lead for the Institute of Neurodiversity, managing 21 countries. So, initially, I wanted to know about what challenges he'd faced when it came to feeling included throughout his career and Silvan told me, 'Once I finally had the proper diagnosis established, I guess, in terms of challenges in workplaces, the biggest one for me was always the hierarchy and narrowed approach to roles. Traditional requirements such as degrees, behavioural job interviews and the requirement to fit in, or not being a "culture fit", were rife for me and left me feeling like an outsider. To put this into perspective, I spent 10 out of my 15+ years of work experience as a freelancer, before moving into the multinational corporate space only as of 2017, with LinkedIn being the largest company I've worked for.'

One thing Silvan noted along the way was that 'neurominorities often tend to be multifaceted and entrepreneurial in terms of interest, expertise and areas they enjoy working in, but others are expertly skilled in a particular area and an equal amount are highly skilled but possessed with a less competitive nature. Same as the neuro-majority, really.'

He continued, 'Overcoming challenges is about asking for help and gracefully accepting it. Then paying it forward to someone else. With me being a deeply value-driven person, I stay true to values, particularly when things get tough. My career was also built organically, and I can intrinsically relate to a diverse group of personalities, having worked my way up from a dishwasher to becoming the Global Lead at the Institute of Neurodiversity (ION) where creating a culture of diversity and inclusion is at our core. I believe the world's problems are based on either miscommunication or ignorance. One's choice is to become part of the solution by solving the former or be the problem by remaining the latter.' A sentiment I wholly agree with!

Silvan's job as the Global Lead at ION is to empower, unite and support the global community in developing diverse and inclusive strategies, country support, scaling up business operations, fundraising, advocacy and by gathering voices to drive policies and changes on a governmental level.

Each of the 21 countries have their local chapter, supported by the global team with resources, programmes and constructive insight as to their needs and challenges and how to overcome them. It's all about co-creation and being intrinsically motivated by purpose.

ION also participated in the 2023 World Health Summit in Berlin, Germany. They were also represented at the World Economic Forum 2024 in Davos, where ION co-launched a hybrid 'neuro-distinct leaders' initiative, gathering 20 global senior neurominority leaders to discuss the year's topics and how to make the World Economic Forum more accessible, diverse and inclusive. They also have a Research and Professional Development Unit in partnership with the University College Dublin where ION run monthly masterclasses and annual conferences on creating an inclusive culture around the subject of neurodiversity. To put this in perspective, all of this has been defined and executed strategically since their inception in October 2021... so they are cooking with gas! That's the true power of a diverse neurodivergent team!

But I wondered, with all this success, when it comes to ION helping companies to evolve culture, how Silvan felt that companies could benefit most from building a more sustainable inclusive culture and strategy.

Silvan said, 'It's not a question of benefit, it's a question of whether companies are aware of and willing to bear the competence of not building a sustainable, inclusive and accessibility-driven company culture.

'The world is changing at an increasingly accelerated pace with many unknown factors and variables influencing and evolving the status quo. Trying to keep things as they are and not injecting diverse perspectives, people and cultures into the business, in my opinion, inevitably will lead to challenges that, if insurmountable, lead to the eventual demise of the said business. However, in the short term, inclusive organizations will see improved efficiency and other metrics but, more importantly, in the long term it creates sustainable, iterative business models and approaches.'

Strong words, but words that I believe in too. So, I wanted to hear from Silvan what his core advice was when it comes to advising a company how to build an inclusive culture. Silvan believes that 'it starts at board and leadership level by way of first assessing the status quo within an organization. Discovering and evaluating their own policies, processes, as well as built-in biases within the business, but also actively engaging with neurominority employees already contributing and adding value to the business, because, surprise, we neurominorities have been around since the beginning, too.

'The sad truth is that a significant number of neuro-distinct individuals are struggling to secure employment. The ones who do succeed often mask, at great expense to their mental and physical health, and these are the ones who know best how to help you design an inclusive, diverse, accessible business by implementing universal design approaches. So, heed your recruitment process!'

Now, as Silvan manages and oversees over 21 countries' representatives and neurodiversity initiatives that vary throughout each region, I wondered how he felt his neurodivergence as an individual lends itself to that type of work. After all, this book is about how neurodiversity can revolutionize your business, right?!

What Silvan told me is, 'My particular cognitive differences help me excel in a few areas: my multilingualism, hyperlexia, adaptability and interconnected thinking on the one hand, with my innate relatability paired with an outgoing personality and above-average dexterity and perseverance on the other hand.

'Hyperlexia describes people who have a tremendous reading-comprehension, often paired with hyper-intuition and eidetic or extensive memory. As an example, I can read, comprehend and retain up to 100 pages of a book within 60 minutes, provided the content stimulates or motivates me emotionally. And that can be very useful when I'm fighting a cause and wading through policy-driven red tape to help change people's lives.'

Silvan also suggested, 'I think that by far my most interesting strength (as I came to realize through recent learning, reading and sharing experiences) is my conceptual synaesthesia. Synaesthesia describes the process of experiencing a particular stimulus in more than one modality. Some of the most commonly known are traits like hearing and smelling colours, but it also extends to spatial sequence and differences in perceiving time or projecting and being able to rotate imaginary mental objects when thinking through creative ideas, and I've found that in exploring this it has truly helped me to really push my boundaries in a range of different projects and initiatives. But with things like this you have to test and trial it, kind of like Harry Potter working on his wizardry, because without practice and focus it's wasted potential talent/value.'

With this in mind, considering his unique approach to company and self-evolution, I wanted Silvan to share with me some examples of the most interesting/innovative neurodiversity initiatives he's seen and why he thought they were effective against traditional efforts to tackle neurodiversity.

Unfortunately, Silvan suggested that 'there hasn't been much innovation in the last few years, but I feel that it is less about being the most innovative rather than ensuring those initiatives are co-created by and for the community, agile and open to changes and adjustments along the way.'

He professed that 'one of the most important aspects to creating an inclusive culture shift is to have constant feedback loops, gathering and analysing data which you need to inform current and new approaches, while including diverse stakeholders from various underrepresented and underserved populations. And with bigger organizations, global initiatives should be informing and supporting local approaches.

'Organizations need to acknowledge that, rather than forcing an old structure into a new design, they need to be holistically decomposing, transforming and reconstructing new ones and emphasizing that and including, actively engaging and acting upon the input of stakeholders with lived experience, not just using their presence as a token.'

Silvan also stated that the most important item to consider, in his opinion, is that 'it is a co-creationary, constant, systemic effort that never ends and neither does the need to become and remain sustainable, inclusive and empathic to pioneer a better future for everyone'.

Examples of good practice

I thought it might be interesting to highlight a few case studies of inclusive workplaces and the successful implementation of an inclusive workplace culture strategy. These include:

- **Salesforce CRM:** Salesforce is renowned for its commitment to equality and inclusivity. The company has implemented a variety of initiatives, including equal pay assessments, employee resource groups and training programmes focused on unconscious bias. Salesforce's commitment to inclusivity is reflected in its high employee satisfaction and retention rates. They also invest in initiatives that support their values, such as acting for racial equality and justice, advocating for equal rights, proactively supporting the LGBTQ+ community, investing in worldwide education on both a local and country to country level, championing supplier diversity by offering resources and education to those they are partnered with and creating access to career opportunities through apprenticeship schemes and other similar initiatives.[3]

- **Accenture:** Accenture has been a leader in creating an inclusive workplace culture for years. The company has set ambitious diversity goals, implemented inclusive leadership training and established programmes to support employees with disabilities. Accenture's commitment to diversity and inclusion has been recognized with various awards and accolades. They provide specialized training, networking support, flexible work arrangements, mentoring, mental health resources, equal benefits to same-sex couples where local law permits and more. They also focus deeply on fostering trust and transparency, so they use measurable goals, share their workforce demographics publicly in key geographies to support awareness and value adoption, and collect data to continuously improve and hold their leaders accountable.[4]

Implementing peer-to-peer support programmes

Another aspect to creating an inclusive culture that is really important for the companies who are looking to become cutting edge when it comes to wellbeing is the implementation of peer-to-peer support programmes. 'Peer-to-peer support', by its definition, is the support given by people who belong to the same group or the people around you within an environment that share the same experience. When it comes to things like mentorship, help would usually be provided by an expert, but in peer-to-peer support everyone is equally valued and qualified to be helping one another. Peer-to-peer support is fundamentally built on sharing a common trust among individuals, and this becomes important because it enables them to express their personal issues that are perhaps difficult to express under the guise of a more traditional mentorship process, as you find with things like mental health first aiders or coaches.

A study from the National Library of Medicine in the US, as with many other studies globally, also suggests that peer-to-peer support is associated with improvements in mental health which include results like greater happiness, better self-esteem and more productivity.[5]

Mental health peer-to-peer support

For several years mental health first aid training certification has lacked governance and the process has become a 'tick box' exercise for many, with hundreds of mental health first aiders burning out consistently from overwhelm. The companies who are most productive in their wellbeing are letting go of this old approach and working towards peer-to-peer support, because it's much more effective and sustainable.

Setting up a mental health peer-to-peer support network within your business is a commendable initiative, as it can contribute significantly to the wellbeing of your employees. A supportive workplace culture fosters mental health resilience and can enhance overall productivity, and peer-to-peer support means that those who are in the business are working better together and better understand each other's needs. Companies need to stop telling people the company is like a family, and instead give their employees the tools to genuinely make it more like one.

A 12-step approach to implementing a mental health peer support network

Working with my clients I am regularly helping them migrate or evolve from simply having some mental health first aiders; here are the essential steps that I always provide them with. These will guide you in establishing an effective mental health peer support network:

1 **Assess the need:** Before initiating the support network, conduct a thorough assessment of the mental health needs within your organization. Surveys, interviews and feedback sessions can help identify the specific challenges employees may be facing.

2 **Leadership support:** Gain support from top leadership. Highlight the positive impact of a mental health support network on employee wellbeing, productivity and organizational culture. Leadership endorsement is crucial for the programme's success.

3 **Create a mental health policy:** Develop a comprehensive mental health policy that outlines the organization's commitment to promoting mental wellbeing. Clearly define the purpose and objectives of the peer support network, emphasizing confidentiality and non-discrimination.

4 **Training for peer supporters:** Provide training for individuals interested in becoming peer supporters. This training should cover active listening skills, empathy, confidentiality and recognizing when to escalate issues to professional mental health resources.

5 **Identify potential peer supporters:** Encourage employees to volunteer as peer supporters. Consider individuals with good interpersonal skills, empathy and a genuine interest in supporting others. Ensure a diverse representation across different departments and levels within the organization.

6 **Establish communication channels:** Set up a secure and confidential communication platform for peer-to-peer interactions. This could include a dedicated email address, a messaging app or regular face-to-face meetings. Ensure that these channels are easily accessible to all employees.

7 **Promote awareness and reduce stigma:** Launch an awareness campaign to de-stigmatize mental health issues. Use various communication channels to educate employees about the importance of mental wellbeing and the availability of the peer support network.

8 **Regular check-ins and events:** Organize regular check-in events to maintain the momentum of the programme. This could involve workshops, guest speakers or informal gatherings to foster a sense of community and support.

9 **Confidentiality guidelines:** Emphasize the importance of confidentiality within the peer support network. Clearly communicate the boundaries of peer supporters and the process for escalating concerns to professional resources when necessary.

10 **Evaluate and adjust:** Continuously evaluate the effectiveness of the support network. Solicit feedback from participants, measure engagement and adjust based on the evolving needs of the organization.

11 **Collaborate with mental health professionals:** Foster collaboration with external mental health professionals. Establish clear pathways for individuals who require professional assistance, ensuring a seamless transition between peer support and professional help.

12 **Celebrate success and share stories:** Acknowledge the positive impact of the peer support network. Celebrate success stories (while maintaining confidentiality) to encourage a culture of openness and resilience.

By following these steps, you can lay the foundation for a robust mental health peer-to-peer support network within your business, promoting a healthier and more supportive workplace environment.

Conclusion

When it comes down to it, if you consider everything that's involved, building an inclusive workplace culture is an ongoing journey that requires dedication, commitment and a holistic approach.

Organizations that prioritize inclusivity clearly not only foster environments where employees feel valued and supported, they also position themselves as leaders in their industries. The benefits as I've described in the context of an inclusive workplace, including enhanced innovation, improved employee engagement and a positive organizational reputation, contribute to sustained success and resilience in today's dynamic business landscape.

By implementing the strategies outlined in this chapter, organizations can create cultures that celebrate diversity, champion equity and cultivate a sense of belonging for every individual. The case studies of successful companies like Salesforce and Accenture also demonstrate that a genuine commitment to inclusivity is emerging globally and that if you want your business to be seen at the forefront of this movement and you're not tackling it by now, then you're already way behind the curve.

Consider inclusivity across the board as you consider your own human ethics... If someone is laid in front of you bleeding, and a bag of money is only 12 steps away attached to a burning rope waiting to drop off a cliff, are you focused on the burning rope and the bag of money? Or do you want to see what it takes to try and save a life?

Everything in DEI, in my opinion, is about ethics. Regardless of the red tape, the disenfranchised board or stakeholders, the straight white male mentality that's holding your business back for fear of change, what are your ethics? Because without understanding our ethics and values we fight for nothing. But there are people in your business right now that need you to fight for them. Is it even worth sitting in a job role at a desk with gravitas if the company that backs us doesn't care? I suggest not.

So while you may lose on a superficial level going out on a limb to fight for DEI, neurodiversity, disability or any other focus that you believe to be cause-worthy, don't hesitate, trust your gut and try to help those around you see how important it is as a moral imperative as a human being to have a stab at changing the world wherever you can and whenever the opportunity presents itself. Your playing small does not serve those around you, so liberate yourself from your personal fear and you will indeed liberate others as your efforts satisfy their needs through tangible and sustainable change.

Notes

1 S Dixon-Fyle, K Dolan, V Hunt and S Prince. Diversity wins: How inclusion matters, McKinsey & Company, 19 May 2020. www.mckinsey.com/featured-insights/diversity-and-inclusion/diversity-wins-how-inclusion-matters#/ (archived at https://perma.cc/VE9H-TGPP)

2 R Walters. The impact of workplace flexibility on productivity, engagement and diversity, Robert Walters, 2023. www.robertwaltersafrica.com/insights/hiring-advice/blog/the-impact-of-workplace-flexibility-on-productivity-engagement-and-diversity.html (archived at https://perma.cc/PX84-RAXM)

3 L Catillo Martinez. Our 2023 annual equality update: Where we are and where we're going, Salesforce, 28 February 2023. www.salesforce.com/news/stories/annual-equality-update-2023/ (archived at https://perma.cc/4UF3-WLVW)

4 Accenture. Our commitment to inclusion and diversity, 2023. www.accenture.com/pl-pl/about/inclusion-diversity-index (archived at https://perma.cc/LC5G-H5JX)

5 J Richard. Scoping review to evaluate the effects of peer support on the mental health of young adults, BMJ Open, 4 August 2022. www.ncbi.nlm.nih.gov/pmc/articles/PMC9358944/ (archived at https://perma.cc/3KYL-8TUY)

PART THREE

Establishing sustainable change

7

Workplace wellbeing hacks

In the dynamic and fast-paced landscape of today's workplaces, prioritizing employee wellbeing is not just a responsibility but a strategic imperative. Rapidly developing and promoting workplace wellbeing not only enhances employee satisfaction and engagement but also contributes to organizational success. So, in this chapter I wanted to dive into the best strategies that companies can employ to swiftly advance workplace wellbeing, fostering a culture of health, happiness and productivity, while also highlighting some of the best individuals and companies in the UK/global wellbeing industry that I would recommend to anyone when it comes to redefining how they do wellbeing or diversity, equity and inclusion.

Before we get into the detail, it's important to understand wellbeing in a deeper context, as the term is used so readily in business that people have seemingly forgotten the fundamentals before they've even scratched the surface, and a weekly office yoga class does not a sustainable wellbeing programme make. We must remember that workplace wellbeing encompasses every aspect of the physical, mental and emotional health of employees within an organization. It goes beyond traditional benefits packages and addresses the overall work environment, including factors such as work–life balance, mental health support and a positive organizational culture. With that in mind, investing in workplace wellbeing not only enhances the employee experience but also results in increased productivity, reduced absenteeism and improved organizational performance, so there is very definitely a fiscal and human return on investment.

15 key wellbeing strategies

Now, before I get into the individuals and companies that I believe you should bring in when you want to evolve your company's wellbeing journey, I thought it would be good to open up with what I find to be the best strategies for rapid development and promotion of workplace wellbeing. There are, however, 15 primary focus points, so buckle up and pay attention, because you may have some of these in place, you may have none or, if you're a really high-flying company, then you may have covered every base, but my aim here is really to simply show you what I as a neurodivergent individual believe to be the primary markers that galvanize the foundations for sustainability in wellbeing-led activity.

1 **Leadership commitment and role modelling:** Ultimately, rapid development of workplace wellbeing begins with a visible commitment and active involvement from your leadership. Leaders need to champion wellbeing initiatives, communicate their significance and lead by example, sharing their stories and their vulnerability. When employees see leaders prioritizing self-care and balance, it sets the tone for a positive and healthy workplace culture. And that's what every business needs.

2 **Flexible work arrangements:** You also have to embrace and implement flexible work arrangements to accommodate the diverse needs of employees, whether it be someone with neurodiversity, a young mother, someone tackling menopause or a family illness. This can include options such as remote work, flexible hours and compressed workweeks. Flexibility enhances work–life balance, reduces stress and contributes to overall wellbeing because it gives us the freedom to tackle the challenges we face outside of work, while not feeling guilty about whether we will be judged as effective or not.

3 **Wellbeing programmes and initiatives:** You can also introduce targeted wellbeing programmes and initiatives that address different aspects of employee health. These could even be led or

championed by your employee resource groups and could include simple and cost-effective things like fitness challenges, mindfulness workshops, mental health resources and nutrition programmes. Rapid implementation of such initiatives demonstrates a commitment to employee wellbeing and provides immediate benefits that will increase productivity and reduce absenteeism.

4 **Regular check-ins and feedback mechanisms:** Establish regular check-ins between employees and their supervisors to gauge wellbeing and be sure that you actually address any concerns raised – don't just say you will do something and then not execute. You can also implement anonymous feedback mechanisms to provide a safe space for employees to share their thoughts. This ongoing communication helps identify issues early on and allows for swift intervention before individual employee wellbeing becomes detrimental for your staff.

5 **Professional development opportunities:** Companies who wish to succeed should provide opportunities for professional development that align with individual career goals. Investing in employee growth and learning contributes to a sense of purpose and fulfilment means that individuals feel seen and valued and investing in understanding what their long-term goals are and could be the difference between losing them and inspiring loyalty. If you try to stimulate more rapid access to relevant training and development resources, you will consistently promote job satisfaction and overall wellbeing.

6 **Promoting work–life balance:** It's easy to encourage and actively promote a healthy work–life balance. Set clear expectations around working hours and overtime, and discourage a culture of constant connectivity, so that people don't feel they will be chastised if they're offline or focused on themselves every now and again. Encouraging employees to take breaks and vacations can also support a sustainable and balanced approach to work.

7   **Mental health support:** Prioritize mental health by offering access to counselling services, employee assistance programmes (EAPs) and resources that promote stress management and resilience. Of course, you can't force staff to engage, but those who wish to be introspective and take action will benefit from having these resources available. Ultimately, it's evident that swift and accessible mental health support contributes to a positive workplace culture that prioritizes the holistic wellbeing of employees.

8   **Recognition and appreciation:** Implement regular recognition programmes to acknowledge and appreciate employees' efforts and achievements. If you leave your employees feeling valued, it contributes to a positive psychological environment and enhances overall work satisfaction. And remember that consistent recognition fosters a culture of appreciation and wellbeing, which invaluable in retaining the right talent.

9   **Health and wellness facilities:** It isn't always feasible to provide health and wellness facilities within the workplace because it depends on the size of your organization, but if it is then do so. This could include on-site gyms, relaxation areas or spaces for meditation and reflection. Even a simple breakout room which people could use for meditation or prayer, or to read some carefully chosen literature, could boost morale. Access to these facilities also encourages employees to prioritize their physical and mental health during the workday.

10 **Inclusive and diverse culture:** Try to foster an inclusive and diverse workplace culture that promotes a sense of belonging. However, developing an inclusive culture involves proactively addressing DEI concerns and this starts by understanding staff needs, again through employee resource groups or peer support initiatives. A diverse workforce actively contributes to a rich tapestry of perspectives, creating an environment where everyone feels valued and supported.

11 **Technology for wellbeing:** Leverage technology to support wellbeing initiatives but choose wisely and look for companies that can give clear and indicative results from previous work, so you don't waste time and money on tech or apps that your

employees won't engage with. But implementing these initiatives, like wellness apps, virtual fitness classes and mental health resources that employees can access easily, will help them to act. The benefit of technology is that it provides a scalable and rapid means to promote wellbeing across the organization. You might also get some data that helps support further budgets or proves your model is working.

12 **Clear communication:** Communicate wellbeing initiatives and resources clearly and consistently. This could be as simple as a monthly wellbeing email that updates staff on what's accessible, shares some inspiring stories and encourages momentum. It also reinforces that your company cares and that you are trying to be proactive. Ensure that employees are aware of the available programmes, support services and the company's commitment to their overall wellbeing. Open and transparent communication also helps your company to foster trust and engagement.

13 **Peer support and networking:** If you facilitate opportunities for peer support and networking, like the implementation of employee resource groups that are focused on wellbeing or create mentorship programmes that allow employees to connect and share experiences, then this peer support will contribute to a sense of community and camaraderie. You will also gain useful insights into how you can improve the lives of your employees and might even find you get some innovation that will improve other areas across the business.

14 **Promoting healthy habits:** This can be done in your wellbeing-backed communications or independently, but you can also encourage healthy habits within the workplace, such as regular breaks, hydration and healthy eating options. Try to focus on creating an environment that supports physical health. You could even go as far as to provide ergonomic workspaces and promote activities that contribute to overall physical wellbeing.

15 **Evaluation and iteration:** This final point is what most companies miss, or forget to implement, but you should regularly evaluate the impact of wellbeing initiatives through surveys, metrics and

feedback. It's then paramount that you use this data to iterate and refine programmes to better meet the evolving needs of employees. A continuous improvement mindset ensures that wellbeing strategies remain effective over time. You won't always get everything right, but ultimately if you are willing to gauge, fail and learn, then you are moving in the right direction. Most companies try to shy away from failure, but we should embrace our learning around things that don't work and throw weight behind what does. Remember, in response to a question about his missteps, Thomas Edison once said, 'I have not failed 10,000 times, I've successfully found 10,000 ways that will not work.' It's a mindset!

Overcoming potential problems

It's all very well if you've got big budgets and you know generally what you're doing or what you want to cover, but what do you do when you've not even begun to understand your company's wellbeing needs, or when you're a big company that's flailing and you need to understand where you stack up against global best practice?

Well, that's where I wanted to highlight some of the individuals and companies that I've worked with over my years in the mental health space, since before it was a popular subject. These individuals and companies will not only support you, but they also won't take advantage of you, and they will give you demonstrable change in short periods of time, through activity that will engage and inspire your employees/teams like you've probably never seen before.

In order to introduce them in the most effective way I've structured some company problem categories and how each individual/company would be suitable for your needs if you have that sort of problem. All of the people and companies that I mention have helped to shape who I am as an individual today. I would trust them with my son and I trust them with my life as a human being. This is why I recommend them. It is not lip service, it is not for financial gain, it is an objective recommendation for people who are ethical, do the job right and the sort of leaders who I genuinely believe long term will create the most sustainable change when it comes to workplace wellbeing.

Problem category 1: You are just starting your workplace wellbeing strategy and don't know what to do

You have a workplace wellbeing strategy but it's ad hoc and probably not sustainable. You're a global company and need to work to certain standards, but you also want to deliver change and it's currently not happening or isn't joined up enough.

Petra Velzeboer is a dynamic, entertaining and practical storyteller who sets about bringing life, laughter and insight companies as she helps them evolve. A global TEDx speaker, psychotherapist, author and CEO of mental health consultancy PVL, her expertise focuses on topics that impact employees, managers and C-suite leadership with the aim of evolving our workplaces and cultures for the new world of work.

With a new angle on wellbeing, Petra's focus on mental health and resilience in a world of change is one that challenges that status quo and instead focuses on positive psychology, elite performance and creating dynamic teams that you will retain as they grow and evolve together. Her hope is to create a future of work that is good for our health and sustainable for long-term success.

I met Petra nearly 10 years ago and we've been friends and worked together ever since. What I like about her is that she's genuine and authentic at the core; however, she has a candid and considered approach to helping companies understand their needs and define their strategy for their vision, action and support – i.e. their vision for their culture, who they need to look after, their wellbeing programmes, etc.; what actions they need to take in moving forward and creating sustainable change; and how those companies underpin those decisions for the long-term success of their wellbeing programmes and employee support programmes.

Her inspiration and motivation come from her unique and compelling story. Petra was born and raised in a notorious cult, so she knows first-hand what a toxic culture feels like and what it takes to build resilience and take responsibility for good mental health. Petra's also known for comparing cults to corporates and has a heavy focus on improving the lives of employees, while educating senior leadership teams and HR or DEI teams.

The reason I am highlighting Petra as the primary solution to this problem category is because I can guarantee she will be effective for companies at any stage of their wellbeing journey and at any scale.

Problem category 2: You want to develop a productive diversity, equity and inclusion strategy but don't know how

You have an DEI strategy, but you're not sure whether it is delivering any value to those who need it. You want to do more to engage and empower diverse employees and you're wondering how.

For this problem category I have two recommendations as to people I think go above and beyond.

The first is a black British-born female called Marteka Swaby, who lives in London and boasts a rich Jamaican heritage. Marteka first trained as a therapist in 1999 as she had always been fascinated with human behaviour and was particularly curious about the impact of race on mental health, so she spent the early part of her career working with addictions, mostly dealing with issues such as drug rehabilitation, and more recently she has explored eating disorders.

Now, despite being widely successful, she still has a number of patients even to this day because she likes to keep herself humble, her experiences very real and remain grounded as a human being.

Marteka would tell you that she didn't have a university degree until she was 33, but, rather interestingly, the year she achieved that degree was also one of the most painful years of her life, as it was filled with loss, trauma and grief, but she still prevailed.

Marteka had always struggled being employed and her last full-time employed role was in consulting. Recognizing so many issues within the workplace surrounding intersectionality and mental health, Marteka decided to forge her own path. Now running a company called Benevolent Health, Marteka has utilized her entrepreneurial spirit to build a successful business with a mission to create happier, healthier workplaces by making mental health more accessible.

Her purpose is to bring a diverse perspective to mental health through coaching and mentoring, to help companies step aside from the one-size-fits-all approach. Her heart is ever readily available, too, for diverse women, and a huge part of her mission is to see more successful women elevated in their career, business and sphere of influence without sacrificing their mental health.

Marteka is not only someone who can add huge value to your business when considering how to implement or improve DEI strategies, but she will also empower diverse women and break down barriers surrounding intersectionality in a way that's humbling, authentic and sustainable for the long term. And this is why I recommend her highly to everyone I work with.

The second is another successful black business leader, hypno-psychotherapist, writer and speaker called Alex Holmes.

Interestingly enough, Alex worked for over five years in tabloid newspapers and eventually left in 2019 after experiencing burnout and struggling with mental health in high-pressure environments. At the time he decided that the healthiest way to tackle this issue was to write a book about how men think about love, belonging and connection, some of the areas that had challenged him. He also set up a weekly podcast called The Recovery Hour where he explores themes around men's mental health and topics on recovery.

Fast-forward to the present day and Alex has become a successful hypnotherapist and psychotherapist, working with busy professionals and leaders. His approach is a fast-growing, deep-work and enriching approach to solution-focused and future-oriented hypno-psychotherapy for professionals who are seeking inner peace, future change, personal liberation and deep mental rewiring for better recovery.

Alex helps people visualize their goals, energize their bodies, naturalize the changes and talk about the things that matter. In his approach, he helps people and teams find clarity, autonomy and control in a world where that is hard to find.

Most of Alex's training continues as he looks to expand who he is and his impact. All of his academic research is surrounding men's and boys' mental health and emotional wellbeing. As such, he works with schools, colleges, universities and companies to create wellbeing programmes and packages to support organizations in improving the mental health of men and boys from under-served and developing backgrounds. This can take the form of multiple structures such as group work, one-on-one sessions and mastermind sessions for managers, leaders and teachers.

Alex is essentially doing for men what Marteka is doing for women, so as a unit they complement each other readily and cover both angles for businesses looking to empower diverse male and female leaders needs within the businesses that support them.

If you're looking at bringing in an objective lens on DEI, diversity and intersectionality across your business, then I'd personally suggest that you team up Marteka and Alex and get the job done right, so that you end up with a strategy and solution that actually delivers some tangible and sustainable change.

Problem category 3: You want to establish company values that stick

You want to engage employees in your values so that they feel more invested in the culture. You want to create bridges and remove barriers in employee communications. You want to reduce stigma surrounding wellbeing or diversity.

My favourite company in the mental health space by far are known as the Abracademy! In fact, when I was just starting out in the wellbeing space as an up-and-coming mental health keynote speaker, I attended an Abracademy magic show at a mental health event and I genuinely believe it changed me in that moment. It gave me an internal belief in myself and my instincts that has stuck with me ever since.

What the Abracademy believe is that 'magical moments' shift people's mindsets towards belief, wonder and possibility. And they do this by following an impactful approach, to ignite, explore, unlock and embed behaviours. Their process is highly interactive and experiential. They're experts at creating learning journeys that bring wows and wonder to learning and development. No death by PowerPoint here! No box-ticking. The Abracademy create safe spaces for reflection and experimentation, for individuals and groups to discover more about themselves and the topic through experience-based learning.

What they do is practical, and they design their sessions with an evidence-based foundation from psychology, neuroscience and professional development in partnership with experts in their field and universities. They take principles, ideas and best practices to create practical exercises, tools and day-to-day tactics that are immediately useful for participants.

The whole concept is about magic being a canvas in that it ignites a learning mindset because it's playful, shifts perspectives and sparks curiosity.

Magic is a very powerful tool for understanding how our minds and brains work, including how we perceive the world, how we behave and how we form beliefs. So, using magic helps us push the boundaries of what people think is possible and work on soft skills like confidence and problem-solving.

In addition to these values, Abracademy has a focus on multicultural sensitivity, because Abracademy is a multi-cultural team with team members in the United Kingdom, southern and northern Europe, North America, South America and Asia Pacific.

The Abracademy learning experiences are designed and delivered with cultural nuances and differences in mind to ensure that their programmes are meaningful to the location. They also deliver their sessions in a range of languages based on country location.

But one thing is for sure… there's always a magician!

The Abracademy has an incredible team of magicians and expert facilitators who deliver their sessions. They call them their 'magilitators'. They also have the skills to hold groups with presence and energy whilst guiding them towards key learning outcomes as defined in line with the needs of the businesses they are working with.

But everything is about continuous learning. Their hybrid learning journeys are designed with a 'digital first' mindset so that the experience is enhanced by digital technology and learning doesn't stop after the workshop. Abracademy provides participants with extended learning after the events they've attended, and it is always there so employees can practice, improve, master and refresh their skills.

They are genuinely the most exciting and refreshing, cutting-edge wellbeing specialists in the world, in my personal opinion.

Another beautiful company to consider bringing in when looking at wellbeing as a whole is ON:SONG, who specialize in improving staff wellbeing and increasing workplace engagement with their inclusive and transformational musical programmes where they help staff build resilience and develop leadership skills through song.

The whole concept was developed in collaboration with senior HR professionals, so that sessions encourage collaboration and cooperation between teams and allow maximum impact around people development.

The ON:SONG style of musical leadership is charismatic, flexible and inspirational, and their musical leaders are chosen for their dynamic and creative approach, with wide-ranging experience gained in high-profile organizations. They are adaptable, with great judgement surrounding character and situational learning, which helps to bring increased engagement and valuable team insights that help your company better steer the ship.

What's interesting about ON:SONG is that they understand that improved organizational performance is driven by bettering the working lives of the individuals within a workforce, and they are experienced in how a choir can strategically feed into this concept, creating stronger and more resilient teams, with better connections between individuals.

I've truly experienced the impact that this sort of activity can have, even on those who say things like 'I don't sing' or 'You won't catch me in a choir', and the results are profound.

ON:SONG also work towards delivering musical programmes, either weekly or one-off, which increase staff retention, improve diversity and inclusion, and help support and innovative HR functions, striving towards a healthier bottom line. They also have a bespoke mobile app supporting regular sessions where they can accelerate learning, boost confidence and make individuals and groups sound better, faster. They only select and arrange a repertoire that moves, excites and challenges, so it won't be anything you have heard your grandma singing in the garden, and this keeps the energy current and interesting for people of all ages.

You never knew your colleagues could sound this good, but the reality is that with ON:SONG, they can! So, look them up and run a session, or have them help you set up your own company choir. It's worth it and if you'd forgive a shameless pun, you'll certainly come away singing their praises!

Problem category 4: You want to understand more about what's accessible to you in the workplace wellbeing space

You want to talk about what your company are proactively doing when it comes to workplace wellbeing, or diversity equity and inclusion, so that others may follow suit.

Make a Difference events are generally seen as the most innovative and forward-thinking events in the UK and Europe; and, when it comes to wellbeing, they are some of the best events in the world.

There are two primary events that I'd recommend having in your calendar every year.

The first is the Watercooler Event in London every April, which is a free-to-attend, two-day exhibition and conference on workplace wellbeing and the future of work. The event brings together the very latest thinking from over 100 experts, alongside actionable and tangible solutions, to holistically support the health, mental health and wellbeing of employees across the UK and globally.

And the second is the Mad World Summit in London every October. The objective at Mad World is to shift the wellbeing conversation up a gear, evolving the conversation from stigma to solutions. By focusing on fresh thinking, Mad World draws in those that have not yet been reached, as well as those looking for ways to bolster commitment to staff mental health, wellbeing and workplace culture.

Both events have thousands of attendees, and every household-name brand is in the room, whether they're exhibiting or speaking about how they do wellbeing. So, both events are a must if you want to keep up to date with who is who in workplace wellbeing and what you could be implementing for yourself or your business that could help to move the needle for change.

The owners of Make a Difference, Mark Pigou and Simon Berger, are two men who picked me up when I was struggling greatly in my life, and they taught me that you can do great and inspiring things that change people's lives without feeling guilty about earning a living off the back of it. I will forever respect where their genuine and self-less mentorship has led me and to now be readily involved with these huge events as a result of that support has been invaluable for the message of being more human that I am looking to share with businesses around the world.

INSIGHT: Building sustainable change in a global company

I spoke to Estelle Jackson the Global Lead for Diversity, Equity and Inclusion at eBay as part of my exploration of hacks for this chapter and I asked her to help me understand how huge companies like eBay define what to prioritize when it comes to diversity, equity and inclusion, so that you have a more sustainable approach to moving the needle for the benefit of your global staff contingent.

What Estelle told me is that 'diversity, equity and inclusion are core to who we are as a company and community at eBay. As a global marketplace bringing together millions of sellers and buyers across more than 190 markets around the world, our purpose is to connect people and build communities that create economic opportunity for all. eBay's DEI approach is focused on four key objectives: increase representation, cultivate a sense of belonging, engage our communities and allies, and build inclusive tech. These objectives helped us create a global strategy that guides us and serves as our DEI North Star. We then look to help bring those objectives to life with a local lens, recognizing every country we are present in has different cultural awareness, religious practices, political views and socio-economic factors that we need to lean in to, to help prioritize what initiatives and programmes we create, and the support needed to make them work. It's a top-down and bottom-up approach – a global strategy that leans into local objectives and data to make sure eBay actively listens to social signals and decides proactively where to lean into it.'

In service of converting conversation to action in these four focus areas, Estelle says that she relies heavily on data, honest employee feedback via surveys and eBay's Communities of Inclusion to accurately represent its employees worldwide. 'We have 11 Communities of Inclusion [eBay's name for Employee Resource Groups] that represent different demographics within the workforce, for example the LGBTQ+ community, caregivers, military and veterans and people with disabilities. They provide invaluable insight into what our employees need, want and wish to focus on, which helps me to create programmes and initiatives that engage and empower our employees. In addition, we have just launched our neurodiverse ERG and are working on policies and standards for this new addition to our Communities of Inclusion.'

Estelle and her colleagues have created DEI action plans with each of the business functions to not only create bespoke goals and drive accountability, but also 'shine a light on areas of focus unique to each group. These are reviewed, measured and discussed regularly with executive buy-in to sustain momentum and make sure employees can see that their voices are being heard, creating a sense of psychological safety to speak up and nurturing a culture of people first and allyship across the business.'

Making sure each employee's voice is heard and valued globally presents unique challenges not only geographically, but also culturally, legally, socially and politically. It's vital to actively listen, recognize uniqueness and lean into uncomfortable conversations and demonstrate sensitive curiosity to build trust and to create programmes and initiatives that are globally relevant with a local lens. Estelle said, 'At eBay we create awareness, build bridges to learning and are constantly developing our culture by celebrating inclusion and what makes each and every one of our employees unique and authentically amazing.

Taking a human-centric approach remains the cornerstone of this work and delivering substantial progress in service of these strategic objectives continues to be vital to eBay's success as a company. But while we have made progress towards our strategic objectives, we are humble enough to know that our journey is far from complete. So, we remain focused on furthering this work and on the road that lies ahead.'

But while all this sounds like a beautiful thing, I was keen to understand from Estelle what she felt had been the most powerful moment for her during her career looking after DEI.

Estelle suggested that she 'grew up in a family unit where uniqueness and authenticity were encouraged. My mother worked as cabin crew for a big transatlantic airline and travelled the world, bringing back amazing trinkets and telling stories from far-off lands. My mum's best friend was gay and couldn't get married in the 80s so I've always been a strong LGBTQ+ advocate. Being cabin crew, her friends were all over the world, from all walks of life. She was a working parent and showed me that being a mother and having a career you love aren't mutually exclusive and I strive to demonstrate that in the job I do. As a working mother and a caregiver to my own children who are both neurodivergent, I see inclusion as part of the DNA of life.' So, it's fair to say Estelle grew up watching her mother's approach and that created a sense of belonging in what she now calls her 'tribe'.

Estelle also mentioned, 'It has always seemed normal and intuitive to me, to be inclusive and celebrate what makes us unique. Bringing different perspectives to the table has always been a given in the roles I've taken on in my career across recruiting, earlier careers, organizational effectiveness and HR business partnering; building a sense of psychological safety to enable people to admit mistakes, question decisions and create high-functioning teams has always been in my wheelhouse.'

But all that changed on 25 May 2020, the day George Floyd was murdered. Estelle was working for a US tech company that had worked really hard to create a culture of belonging. People felt safe to speak up. They knew how to join an ERG and call out bad behaviour. They were well versed in allyship and bringing their authentic selves to the workplace. But no one was prepared for the repercussions of that day.

Estelle said that she 'woke up on the Tuesday morning to an email from my executives asking what they should do. The most senior people in my global business were asking me for help. It was surreal.' She continued by telling me that so many thought were racing through her mind. 'What should I say? What can I do? Should I post on social media? Should we "black square" our socials for Black Tuesday?

How do we support employees through this? I was afraid I'd say the wrong thing. I didn't want to get this wrong.' Estelle panicked initially, with so many options running through her mind, until it became fundamentally clear to her that her most senior people in the business wanted to do the right thing. They wanted to demonstrate allyship, they wanted to take a stand, they wanted to be seen as educated and knowledgeable. But they weren't sure how. And they didn't want to get it wrong, either.

That drove a measurable change in how DEI was viewed at a global level. Estelle was given a seat at the table to become a catalyst for change. She was given responsibility and accountability to use the Black Lives Matter (BLM) movement that we saw erupt as a result of Mr Floyd's murder, as a catalyst for change. 'That DEI survey that legal had been reticent to approve me sending out to ask employees sensitive questions that could help drive initiatives and education? Approved. Each executive taking a project on with a specific DEI focus that they might not have volunteered for before? No problem!'

And things really did change. 'We saw retention rates increase. We heard in our surveys what employees wanted, how they wanted to identify and what they needed to thrive in the business. Programmes were created and costs covered. Education and awareness workshops were formalized and were part of the quarterly company calendar globally, with executives showing up and being vulnerable. Our senior leaders were held accountable, and their executives led by example in showing up for their ERGs and events.'

The changes we've seen in the world since the BLM movement have, in Estelle's mind, 'catalysed a need for change. For people to learn. Be more aware. Be sensitively curious. To educate themselves and form opinions based on things broader than their own personal frame of reference. And that can only serve to make the world a more inclusive, diverse, tolerant and equitable place to be.'

So, with that in mind, I thought I'd ask Estelle for some insights into innovations/initiatives that eBay have set up to support staff, that have worked really well and why she felt they were successful, with a mindset that perhaps those who read this book can take it upon themselves to try similar things.

What Estelle told me was that 'nurturing a sense of belonging is sometimes thought of as giving everyone equal access: equal access to opportunities, equal access to participate in events, equal access to leaders. But for the majority of people, it is equity, a level playing field, that makes them feel valued and like they belong in an organization as an individual with individual needs.

'Setting up initiatives that create equity in our business is a big part of the DE&I team's role and one that I get the most pleasure out of seeing come to life. Our Pride COI, which focuses on engaging, encouraging and empowering the Lesbian, Gay, Bisexual, Transgender, Queer+ community, came to me last year with feedback. They wanted to point out that although we have an equal opportunities and equality policy, we didn't have anything that stated how we treat people going through any sort of gender expression or transition process. We didn't have a process employees could consult to update their pronouns on their work badge, for example.

'The support this group needed for this particular life event, before, during and after transition, for example, is unique to the LGBTQ+ community and the COI really felt eBay should acknowledge their needs and perspective. So, I created a global working group with experts from all over the business, covering People Experience, Employee Relations, Facilities, Legal and members of the trans community who volunteered to give their perspective on what gender expression and transitioning meant and felt to them.

'This created a truly unique group of subject matter experts willing to look at processes like changing the photo on your employee badge to reflect your style, or which bathroom an employee going through transition should use, what name should appear on someone's email convention and how to approach the subject of transitioning and pronouns with team members. Our People Experience team received an education workshop with Stonewall (an LGBTQ+ charity aimed at supporting and empowering the LGBTQ+ community) to help them best support employees asking for help, or managers needing support with helping a team member going through any form of gender identity or expression change. All of this not only resulted in the gender expression and identity standard we have published on our internal hub for employees to learn about; it also encouraged a sense of belonging in the LGBTQ+ community within eBay and positive sentiment of employees feeling like they can truly bring their authentic selves to the workplace.'

It really is quite inspiring what Estelle and eBay have been doing on the DE&I front, and it certainly provides insight into what a high level of best practice could look like, not to mention the open-minded approach to adaptive change.

Examples of good practice

When it comes to 'doing' wellbeing in a positive way, eBay is not the only company leading the charge, there are a number of companies who are openly sharing their innovation. I wanted to highlight a few who are perhaps more recognizable just to give readers a gauge of what's going on in the industry. Here are some case studies covering successful implementation of 'rapid workplace wellbeing strategies':

- **Google:** Google is renowned for its comprehensive approach to employee wellbeing. The company offers a range of wellness programmes, including on-site fitness centres, mindfulness workshops and access to mental health resources. Google's commitment to employee wellbeing is reflected in its positive workplace culture and high employee satisfaction.[1]

- **Zoom Video Communications:** As a company that experienced rapid growth, Zoom prioritized employee wellbeing during the global shift to remote work. The company introduced initiatives such as virtual wellness events, flexible work schedules and additional time off to support its employees during challenging times. This rapid response contributed to maintaining a positive and supportive workplace culture.[2]

- **Salesforce:** Salesforce has consistently invested in employee wellbeing, especially during times of change and uncertainty. The company offers mental health resources, wellbeing challenges and initiatives to promote work–life balance. Salesforce's commitment to employee wellbeing aligns with its core values, contributing to a positive and inclusive workplace.[3]

It's all moving the narrative in the right direction, especially when companies are trying to be more transparent as to the fundamentals they address when tackling DEI or wellbeing-focused initiatives, because it gives organizations, maybe like the companies attached to the readers of this very book, who don't have the capacity, budgets or capability to define robust and sustainable strategies the opportunity to try something new and build on the ideas off the back of industry giants who are seemingly doing things the right way.

And that's what this book is about, really – insights, honesty and open-minded approaches to trying new things and thinking differently about how we look after one another in society and in business.

INSIGHT: Organizational support for neurodiverse staff

I was really lucky in the development of this book to link up with another inspiring industry leader called Angus Blair, who is the Neurodiversity Lead at Google, to talk to him about living with epilepsy and dyslexia and understand a little more about his journey and what he's learned working in the wellbeing space, especially given his current role with a focus on championing neurodiversity across the Google landscape.

What's poignant for me is that my cousin struggled for years throughout higher education and in the world of work because of her epilepsy, something that most people won't even realize is a neurodiversity in itself, as I outlined in my first chapter, and it took her years to find her fit, gain the confidence to be open about her needs and furthermore forge a career where she is supported and happy. So, it's inspiring to me that Angus has managed to do the same and that now he has the opportunity to make an impact for others. This is why I wanted him involved in this chapter, to help others fast track some of their thinking.

My initial interest was to understand Angus's experience of how companies generally perceive neurodiversity and where he felt that companies are generally lacking, in their pursuit to support neurodivergent employees. After all, many are lacking, but as you'll have seen from a number of my interviews so far, that it's very often similar problems that tend to crop up again and again.

Angus suggested, 'Neurodiversity is slowly becoming something more recognized on an industry level, as the demystifying of the subject becomes more normalized. That said, it is still very stigmatized, with a large proportion of individuals and businesses not knowing what comes under the term neurodiversity and the subsequent fear of trying to address such a broad subject. This is realistically why your book will help so many.

'From my personal experience it is a subject people are happy to acknowledge but at the same time they are totally unaware of how to support it. Those who are neurodiverse can often bring rare and unique skills. These are often leveraged within many types of business and if this can bring success then people are also happy to accommodate success, but it is less tolerated when it comes to support for neurodivergent people through the discovery process (it's almost expected that they should have done the work themselves before they applied for the job), as this sometimes can yield the impression of individuals underperforming along the way, and that's simply not the case. There are just considerations to be made when attracting and maintaining neurodivergent individuals and leaders.'

But Angus went on the tell me, 'Companies can transform this very easily with three simple steps. First, as always, is educating. You can't help or change anything until you know what it is. One neurodiverse person is not the same as the next – dyslexia presents very differently to ADHD so you can't treat them as the same. The second step is leadership. I have been fortunate to have come across some amazing leaders and the uniform thing they have brought to the party is empathy and engaging with me to empower me, in turn helping me to empower them with my skills and knowledge. When you treat someone as an equal you will be surprised where that individual can add value. Third, and finally, accommodations do not have to be big. They can be free and small but making them can transform the average into the exceptional.'

Angus thinks of himself as lucky to be able to have an impact in support of others with neurodivergent needs, so I was keen to know more about the biggest challenges he'd faced vocationally when looking after the needs of other neurodiverse employees.

What he told me was that 'neurodiverse individuals are exceptionally passionate, which is amazing to witness, and my role is to channel that passion productively to maximize our outcome as a business. However, passion, when it's under-utilized, or not channelled properly, or not supported by leadership, can sometimes not be productive, so it is paramount to act as a partner to your neurodivergent individuals and help fuel the passion in as constructive a way as possible.'

As the conversation progressed, I felt it would be interesting to know what the most effective initiatives were that Angus had seen in the workplace wellbeing space when it comes to looking after the needs of neurodiverse staff. I felt that this could give you as a reader some insight into what might be successful straight out of the gate.

Surprisingly, he was adamant that the answer was short but sweet and he told me, 'Communities within communities who can talk and express themselves, knowing full well that they are supported and who are happy to support others, is the most effective way to inspire and instigate sustainable change.' So, it seems that initiatives like the employee resource groups and peer-to-peer support, which have been highlighted a number of times in the previous chapters, are where Angus has seen the biggest impact throughout his career to date.

For me, the issue also rolls back to what can be measured, because if a company can't quantify what they're investing their time and money in then no well-meaning initiative will ever build momentum, and it felt like it would be poignant to ask Angus his opinion on what measured fundamentals companies should employ to better cater for the needs of their neurodiverse staff.

As Angus worked at Google, I expected some tech or analytical tools as his suggested response, but I found his reply more interesting because it was less expected and far more human. He told me, 'When we talk about measured fundamentals, I feel this is a very interesting topic. But I would honestly like to dream big and imagine that one day every company would tackle wellbeing from the standpoint that it's more about being a decent human being and working with people rather than pushing for an outcome, or a fiscal return on investment.

'If a company wants to improve their culture and environment for neurodiverse individuals and they want to measure it, then perhaps firstly start by measuring the education and then measure how many leaders are actually educated and aware of the needs of their neurodivergent staff. If you start by trying to measure your neurodivergent population then you risk tokenizing, and ultimately the results will always be skewed and won't reflect the reality of either your current climate or the potential you might be able to harness.'

I've seen so many people trying to crack the concept of assessing fiscal and human return on investment off the back of all sorts of wellbeing projects, and for me Angus hits the nail on the head. We should be educating ourselves, companies should be educating their leaders and ultimately big businesses, as much as any business, should be tackling initiatives like wellbeing, neurodiversity and DEI, from a perspective that it's the right thing to do and that inevitably if you honour your people, they will inevitably be happier, more effective and more loyal, and that means the bottom line will always improve incrementally.

I mentioned before that my cousin has faced various challenges throughout her life living with epilepsy, so I wanted to come back to this point with Angus to understand whether he felt that he'd been supported throughout his career to date, or whether, as others I've interviewed have mentioned, it had been his job to educate those around him. But I was also keen to find out what challenges he had experienced throughout his working life and what companies could do better in support of this unique neurodiversity, because I feel it's generally rarely recognized.

Angus unfortunately gave an answer not dissimilar to most neurodivergent individuals I've spoken to about neurodiversity in their working life, or those I've interviewed in previous chapters for this book: he stated, 'Absolutely not. Throughout most of my career I've never been supported with my epilepsy (or even my dyslexia for that matter), and I have spent a large chunk of time hiding it and avoiding even discussing it in the workplace. Especially when I have struggled with cluster seizures that leave me mentally exhausted, which then plays right into the hands of my dyslexia, because I can't focus. But now (and this is something that readers can consider within their businesses) I have started self-advocating more and educating others around me. Recently, I built a slide deck that I share with teammates, to educate people across the business, but I also keep it light-hearted – more of an informed situation and any actions they might need to undertake in an emergency. I also found that adding in a quiz at the end, where we have fun guessing the famous celebrity who has epilepsy, really helps people remember it and allows people to feel comfortable talking to me about it rather than it being seen as a sensitive or taboo topic.'

I think what Angus is doing to self-advocate and support colleague with education surrounding his epilepsy is unique. However, it strikes me as frustrating that most of the neurodivergent people that I know have to self-advocate. I rarely meet advocates and allies at senior leadership level, but it would be nice for companies to advocate education surrounding these subjects to support staff. With epilepsy, it's not just a neurodiversity, it's also something that could kill you quite easily if those around you are not aware of the need to do simple things like keeping you from swallowing your tongue or making sure you're safe and not in harm's way, such as falling into furniture if you suddenly have a seizure. So, we need to educate everyone, just as we do with basic first aid if someone in your team or business has this type of condition to manage.

But, coming back to neurodiversity as an overarching theme and knowing that many of you reading this may still be at the start of your journey embracing neurodiversity, I wanted to know from Angus what, in his experience, he feels could be the most detrimental effect if companies don't embrace neurodiversity across their organization and what would be the first thing that he recommends people should do to support neurodiversity if the business is just starting out on this valuable initiative.

What he said was, 'This is the key – failing to embrace neurodiverse individuals means companies will get left behind, the brand value drops the revenue drops and you lose, all because you didn't adapt or listen. If I was starting out setting up a business, I would make it clear that we embrace all job applications, regardless of any level of diversity in the candidates, and would offer as much support as possible, as part of our leadership commitment to the employees and our business. However, it would need to be a partnership – we'd need to work closely with those individuals to give them the most value and in kind gain the most value from them, not just provide lip service. To solve problems, we need to look at things from all angles, so your neurodivergence brings a new angle which won't always have been explored before.'

Conclusion

In addition to what you've seen in this chapter, ultimately, I feel off the back of my work to date and the explorations throughout this book so far that rapidly developing and promoting workplace wellbeing is an investment that pays dividends in the context of employee satisfaction, engagement and organizational success. It is only by adopting a multifaceted approach that encompasses leadership commitment, flexible work arrangements, targeted wellbeing programmes and continuous evaluation that companies can create environments where employees thrive and contribute to the best of their ability. In fact, Deloitte even did a study that suggested 'for every £1 spent on supporting the mental health and wellbeing of their workforce, employers get (on average) about £4.70 back in increased productivity'. Which means that the evidence is clearly there to suggest that investing in wellbeing is paramount to companies achieving more, not only for their people, but also for their bottom line.[4]

The case studies of successful companies I mentioned, like Google, Zoom and Salesforce, illustrate the positive impact of prioritizing wellbeing, especially during times of change and uncertainty. Overcoming challenges and ensuring sustained wellbeing involves ongoing assessment, feedback mechanisms, flexibility and a holistic perspective that considers the interconnected dimensions of employee health at the core of any strategy.

As organizations continue to adapt to evolving work environments, those that prioritize and rapidly advance workplace wellbeing will be better positioned to attract and retain top talent, foster a positive organizational culture and navigate the challenges of today's dynamic business landscape.

That being said, the journey toward workplace wellbeing is not a destination but a continuous evolution, reflecting a commitment to the ongoing health and happiness of every individual within the organization. If you do not take this seriously as a business, then you should not be surprised if your employees do not take you seriously.

Notes

1 K Ganesh. Why is Google's culture this amazing: 10 secrets you should know about their culture and get inspired from, Culture Monkey, 14 November 2023. www.culturemonkey.io/employee-engagement/googles-culture/ (archived at https://perma.cc/Q7SH-729H)

2 C Farrow. Zoom: Employee wellbeing boosted with benefits, Make a Difference, 16 December 2020. makeadifference.media/newsletter/zoom-employee-wellbeing-boosted-with-benefits/ (archived at https://perma.cc/Z7Y5-A824)

3 Salesforce. FY24 stakeholder impact report, 2024. www.salesforce.com/content/dam/web/en_us/www/documents/white-papers/salesforce-fy24-stakeholder-impact-report.pdf (archived at https://perma.cc/V3WR-ZD5C)

4 Deloitte. Poor mental health costs UK employers £51 billion a year for employees, 2024. www.deloitte.com/uk/en/about/press-room/poor-mental-health-costs-uk-employers-51-billion-a-year-for-employees.html (archived at https://perma.cc/N9MX-Y3SM)

8

Championing neurodiversity

Championing neurodiversity in business is crucial for numerous reasons that extend beyond mere compliance or social responsibility. I've already talked about how embracing neurodiversity unlocks a vast pool of untapped talent while fostering a culture of innovation/ creativity and improves team dynamics/performance while enhancing employee engagement and satisfaction. But in addition to these core benefits, championing neurodiversity is not just about upgrading your internal operations; it also positively impacts your external reputation and customer relationships. Companies that prioritize diversity and inclusion, including neurodiversity, are viewed more favourably by consumers, investors and other stakeholders, so by demonstrating a commitment to diversity and inclusion you can enhance your brand reputation, attract top talent and build stronger connections with your customers, all while you're doing the right thing to improve the working environment for your employees. It's a no brainer!

Championing neurodiversity internationally

I've talked a lot in the book so far about what companies can do on a local level when looking at the strategy for wellbeing, neurodiversity or diversity-led initiatives. However, I think it's also important to review some core aspects surrounding what companies who have an international presence in multiple countries have to consider when looking to evolve.

Of course, all my comments, my interviews, research and suggestions work for most companies, but when you have international sites, varying cultural dynamics and you have to join the dots, there needs to be a foundation. So, here's where I stand on championing neurodiversity internationally:

1 **Culture:** You have to start by looking at cultural sensitivity and adaptation, because companies operating internationally must be attuned to cultural variations in attitudes towards neurodiversity and wellbeing. Championing neurodiversity on a global scale requires a nuanced understanding of local perceptions and practices related to cognitive differences.

2 **Legal aspects:** Then you must consider legal compliance and local regulations, because complying with local regulations and legal frameworks related to neurodiversity and wellbeing is crucial regardless of the target country. Companies should and must be aware of any specific laws or requirements in each country of operation and adapt their policies and practices accordingly.

3 **Communication:** Next up are considerations around multilingual communication, because ensuring neurodiversity initiatives are communicated effectively across linguistic and cultural boundaries is essential to building sustainable global best practices. Companies should invest in multilingual communication strategies to reach all employees, fostering a sense of inclusivity.

4 **Support services:** You need to have the capacity for customizing support services, because neurodiversity support services should address the specific needs and cultural contexts of each international location. This may even involve collaborating with local experts and organizations to ensure the effectiveness and cultural relevance of support programmes, so that they maintain momentum and engagement.

5 **Training:** It's also worth implementing global training programmes across the business, because if you develop and implement global training programmes that incorporate cultural sensitivity and adaptability, you will gain more credibility for what you are

looking to achieve. Training should also be designed to resonate with diverse audiences, fostering a shared understanding and commitment to neurodiversity across the company's international footprint.

6 **Leadership:** And finally, there should be diversity in the context of your leadership representation, because if you promote diverse leadership that reflects the international scope of the company, then leaders from various backgrounds will contribute to a more inclusive decision-making process and serve as role models for employees across different regions. This will further underpin your company's values towards inclusion, and foster loyalty and engagement from employees.

Examples of good practice

A few companies who seem to have got this right and that I consider to be exemplary when it comes to championing neurodiversity in the workplace are the following:

- **JP Morgan Chase:** JP Morgan Chase has embraced neurodiversity through its Autism at Work programme. The initiative aims to hire individuals on the autism spectrum for various roles within the company. JP Morgan Chase provides specialized training, mentorship and accommodations to support the success of neurodivergent employees.[1]

- **IBM:** IBM has a longstanding commitment to diversity and inclusion, including neurodiversity. The company's Autism at Work programme aims to hire individuals on the autism spectrum for roles in software testing, programming and other technical fields. IBM provides extensive training, support and accommodations to ensure the success of neurodiverse employees in the workplace.[2]

- **Santander UK:** Santander UK has implemented its Neurodiversity Programme to support individuals with neurodiverse conditions in the workplace. The programme provides training, support and accommodations to help neurodiverse employees excel in their roles.[3]

- **Google:** Google's Autism at Work programme is dedicated to hiring individuals on the autism spectrum for positions across the company. Google offers specialized training, support and accommodations to ensure the success of neurodiverse employees in the workplace.[4]

Helping businesses develop their strategies and practices

As part of this chapter, I wanted to interview some individuals whose companies help businesses develop their neurodiversity activity for a living. I thought it would be important for people to not only read about what companies I'd recommend if I was starting the neurodiversity strategy journey from scratch, but also have a bit more insight as to how they actually practise what they preach.

INSIGHT: Unlocking the power of neurodiversity – Thriiver

My first candidate was Lawrence Howard, the CEO of a company called Thriiver who are experts at helping individuals and organizations build better businesses by providing them with tools and training so that they can reach their true potential. What Thriiver have been doing for over 26 years now is helping organizations create inclusive workplaces for the benefit of everyone by showing them how to understand and unlock the power of neurodiversity and disability in the workplace.

Their clients include the NHS, HMRC, BBC, Lloyds TSB, Logica, HMPS, Tesco, Grant Thornton and beyond, so they're clearly doing something right. Knowing Lawrence personally and having seen the company grow into arguably the longest-standing business in the UK devoted to neurodiversity and disability, I wanted delve deeper into what it is that Thriiver does that makes the business so successful.

Lawrence told me, 'Initially when I launched Thriiver, the focus was on assistive technology to help disabled people in the workplace, but soon afterwards we started to wrap other services around the tech as this was needed to provide a more comprehensive solution to clients. I therefore employed additional new people who could help with training and coaching which I then blended into our offering according to the individual's needs. In other words, some people only needed the technology and training on how to use it, while others needed only coaching – but most needed elements of all three.'

He added, 'Over the past 10 years, businesses have become increasingly aware of the talents and abilities that neurodivergent employees can bring to the workplace. They are great problem solvers, are able to simplify complex tasks, be creative, keep their businesses ahead of their competitors and as a consequence boost the bottom line of the businesses that they work in. So, I have been driven by my passion to help disabled people in the workplace as a result of my own experiences with severe dyslexia. As Thriiver has grown I have been able to spend more time educating C-suite managers on the benefits of having a neurodiverse workplace, often by measuring and showing them the differences their staff make once the right support has been put in place. This has led us to deliver management awareness training to organizations to help them understand how to unlock this talent within their own workforce as well as when recruiting. It also massively helps staff retention when people are able to use their abilities to their fullest and see the results that they can achieve.'

Lawrence believes that their success has been due to the fact that they have 'constantly evolved and adapted to the changing needs of people and businesses, as well as the increasing understanding of how being neurodiverse can be a big advantage in so many ways'.

But I wanted to understand a little more about what Lawrence, as an openly neurodivergent CEO (who has built a business off the back of helping others with their diversity, equity and inclusion initiatives) feels are the biggest challenges that companies currently face when looking to tackle neurodiversity for the first time.

Lawrence suggests, 'There are two main challenges that I believe businesses are currently facing. Firstly, the education system is totally outdated. It focuses on rote learning of facts and figures that have no relevance once you leave education. It crushes creativity and curiosity and treats neurodiversity as a disability. This impacts the way that people view neurodiversity because they are told all through education that it's a problem. Secondly, those businesses that are recognizing the abilities that neurodiverse people can bring really don't know where to start.'

Lawrence continued, 'We are entering a new phase in the world with technology, including AI, changing the way we work. These changes are even more profound than those of the Industrial Revolution in the mid-18th to 19th centuries. These changes are happening really rapidly, and they require businesses to think very differently about how they define job roles and how the workplace should operate. Many are still operating in a way that was more relevant 50 years ago than today, and it's really difficult to change when it's all you've known. However, with around 15–20 per cent of the workforce being neurodiverse, neurodiverse people can be the ones who transform your business today and into the future, and the businesses that are recognizing this are already proving to be the most successful on both a local and a global level.'

This harks back to the studies from the likes of McKinsey and the *Harvard Business Review* that I mentioned in earlier chapters, which were proving the same concept.

It's interesting to me that Lawrence being dyslexic means that he's had to think differently all his life and that's eventually led to running Thriiver and solving problems that will help evolve or change thousands of lives as the years go on and the company grows. This made me wonder how his personal journey with dyslexia has helped him in business and made Lawrence so successful at what he does. Lawrence said, 'It's given me a passion to help others and enables me to see the big picture and also work out how to solve problems, both for clients and within my own business. I can see things that aren't working well and can reorganize the way that things are done by getting under the skin of the problem and finding solutions that others can't see. However, probably more importantly, my own experiences have led me not just to want to help, but to break new ground and be the very best at what I do.'

So, there Lawrence mentioned that he works out the problems for his own staff as well as clients, but I wanted to know how Lawrence, as an expert, personally manages the wellbeing of his own staff and how he feels that directly impacts the business. What he told me was, 'The important thing is to know your team, understand them, listen to them, trust them and in return they'll trust you, feel valued and be motivated. It's important to create a culture where people feel safe to try things out and not to worry if it doesn't work first time. This culture will encourage ideas and innovative ways of doing things. If the ideas or solutions are good then you must implement them, if they're not good or need refinement then you must explain why without making people feel it was wrong to suggest the idea in the first place. And I believe that if you hold true to this sort of value system then you will be able to underpin sustainable development surrounding your overarching staff wellbeing.'

Obviously, dealing with businesses tackling neurodiversity and disability every day means that you are likely to see a wide range of problems, but I thought it might be insightful to find out from Lawrence what he felt were the most prevalent pain points that businesses were struggling with when they knocked on the door to ask for his help, and how he helps them to tackle these issues. Lawrence suggested that it usually starts with one of the following issues: 'We've got a member of staff. We know that they're capable, but they are failing to deliver.' 'We're having problems with retention of staff. We have a huge turnover but don't know how to address it.' 'We recognize that we need to do better with diversity, equity and inclusion. We understand that there are benefits as we've seen other businesses get it right, but we just don't know where to start.'

However, just as each person is different, so is each business. But Lawrence said, 'My team and I will always start by trying to understand the existing culture within the business and their sector, their direction of travel and what they want to achieve. This understanding will then form the basis for what we suggest are the priorities and where they can get some quick wins to help everyone start seeing the benefits.'

Most importantly, Lawrence told me, the fundamentals that every business should consider when tackling the subject of neurodiversity for the first time are:

- Create an environment of psychological safety so that employees feel able to speak up.
- Listen to them when they do speak up!
- Make changes based on the feedback – even if it's uncomfortable.
- Leave your ego outside the office.

'These core pillars are those that I believe are absolutely fundamental when trying to implement a framework that will stand the test of time and genuinely improve the lives of company employees. They are simple, but not easy!'

INSIGHT: Supporting neuro-inclusive businesses – Lexxic and Cognassist

This leads me to introduce another individual I thought would make an interesting interview for this chapter – an inspiring woman called Georgina Kennedy. Georgina is unique in so many ways, not least because she has had both an ADHD and dyslexia diagnosis, but also because she's a proud member and advocate of the LGBTQ+ community, she's ranked among the top 50 female neurodiversity advocates in the UK, and she also works for a company that delivers change to businesses through digital cognitive assessments that helps employers support their neurodivergent staff.

As such an impressive female leader, I was interested to learn more about Georgina and her company, but I was also interested initially to understand what the most common misconception relating to her neurodiversity was, and how Georgina felt that this was holding back her career before joining Cognassist.

Georgina felt that 'one of the most common misconceptions is that ADHD is simply a lack of focus. In reality, ADHD is a complex neurodevelopmental disorder that involves difficulties with attention, hyperactivity and impulse control. Another misconception is that ADHD is a childhood disorder that individuals outgrow. However, many people continue to experience symptoms into adolescence and adulthood, although they may manifest differently. My GP told me at 19 that ADHD didn't exist in adults, hence I ended up not being professionally diagnosed until I was 35 years old.'

She stated that 'some people mistakenly believe that individuals with ADHD are lazy or not trying hard enough, when in reality ADHD is a legitimate medical condition that affects the brain's executive functions. There's also a misconception that medication alone can cure ADHD. While medication can be a helpful component of treatment, it is usually part of a more comprehensive approach that may include therapy, lifestyle changes and support, and that's certainly the route I've taken.'

Another thing that Georgina told me in respect of her dyslexia is that 'this too is often misunderstood as a visual issue, such as seeing letters backward, but realistically, dyslexia is a language-based learning disability that affects a person's ability to read, write and spell.

'I was often told that people with dyslexia are not intelligent, and for me that means there's a misconception that individuals with dyslexia have lower intelligence. However, this is completely false; dyslexia is not related to intelligence and many individuals with dyslexia have average or above-average intelligence. And I was also told that my dyslexia can be outgrown with enough practice, but in fact it is a lifelong condition. However, by implementing appropriate support and interventions, individuals like me with dyslexia can develop effective strategies to cope with challenges.'

Before joining Cognassist, some of the things that impacted Georgina consisted of:

- Insomnia has been a huge issue all of her life – Georgina now takes antihistamine every night along with melatonin.
- Rejection sensitivity dysphoria (RSD) – perceived rejection, which can be crippling a work and at home.

- Emotional dysregulation, especially at work around her hormonal cycle – this worsens during menopause. It's like being on drugs – huge highs and lows, never calm.
- Crying to regulate frustration can be shocking for those who are unaware.
- Imposter syndrome – not feeling like she's good enough and having huge doubts.
- Intrusive thoughts, where Georgina was petrified of dying for years – now she just blocks it out but it took 20 years for it to stop.
- Racing thoughts and a need to always be doing something.

Some of these are also generally things that Georgina will face longer term until she is able to best understand and approach possible coping mechanisms. However, she states that 'those that hold me back in the context of work have partially been managed because of the work that my company Cognassist do and also how they approach looking after me and cultivating all of the inspiring and wonderful things about me as a human being, including my insightful and intelligent approach to work.'

This line of questioning led me to want to understand what it is that Cognassist actually does as a company, so that I could best understand if it was an initiative worth championing and recommending to readers and the organizations that I work with.

What Georgina told me was that Cognassist is a SaaS company that has created a neuro-inclusion platform for businesses which includes:

- **Neuro-inclusion certified training:** The training ensures that a workforce is equipped to comfortably navigate neurodiversity, fostering an environment of openness and proactive support. Businesses can empower their team with Cognassist's City and Guilds certified training to enable neuro-inclusion, through e-learning and webinars. They also provide certified training for employees, managers and neurodiversity champions.

- **Cognitive mapping:** Another aspect of Cognassist is that they provide world-leading cognitive mapping that is clinically robust. The cognitive mapping doesn't result in labels, even for those with a neurodiversity; it shows people their natural processing bias and thinking differences, because you can't compare one person to another, so it's more individualistic. This is about enabling every employee to understand their own cognition, and act on it to thrive and to develop a deeper understanding of cognitive diversity and neurodiversity.

- **Personalized workplace adjustments:** Cognassist also offers tailored adjustments and strategies for both employees and their managers, carefully curated based on disclosure, job role and cognitive results, which enables teams by providing adjustment strategies for everyone.

- **Neuro-difference disclosure framework:** There are diverse preferences for disclosure, so Cognassist's approach also goes beyond the binary where they offer tailored options, acknowledging that individuals may want different levels of disclosure, providing a nuanced and inclusive experience. This information is then handled under a legal wrapper and only shared with explicit permission-based controls to ensure privacy and confidentiality.

So, all in all, the Cognassist organization seems to underpin a lot of the fundamentals surrounding where we should be going in moving away from the 'one-size-fits-all' approach I mentioned in previous chapters. It's tackling these issues surrounding individuality and using science to give a more definitive understanding of an individual's cognitive needs.

That said, you will always have triggers, personal preferences and things that make you uncomfortable that can't necessarily be measured or defined through software or tools, so I am interested to see how the analytics relating to anxiety peaks, etc., will relate to the nuance of how we act or our coping mechanisms as neurodivergent human beings. They are certainly a company worth talking to, though.

Georgina mentioned, 'Before working with a company that wanted to champion my neurodiversity, I felt lost and without hope. I had originally joined the wellbeing industry because I was struggling, and I wanted to be out and proud. I just wanted to do something that made me feel I could help others be their true selves.

'Initially I joined a company called Lexxic (a psychological consultancy that helps organizations develop environments in which neurodiversity can thrive) when I was at rock bottom, going through therapy after the poor treatment by my previous employer. The silly thing about it all is that I was too ashamed to tell them the truth, but this mindset is like so many others who are neurodiverse and you just feel stupid.

'What I love about working with a neurodiversity business is that they change lives for the better, they help organizations to understand the value of neurodiverse minds and help employers to empower and unlock the unique talents of neurodiverse employees. But what I loathe is that so many companies still don't have the right support in place, nor do they have an inclusive working environment, or in many cases the inclination to bother.'

Georgina originally bumped into Lexxic at an event and saw the words dyslexia and neurodiversity on their poster. Being impulsive, she walked up to them and said, 'I am neurodiverse. If you want a salesperson, I am your woman.' She then left her number and got a call the following week, and the rest is history.

Georgina wanted to change her negative experience and negative mindset into a positive one and she wanted to be open and to be able to disclose her neurodivergence to her employer so that she could be free and bring her whole self to work. Recognizing that we spend more time at work than anywhere else, Georgina felt that 'it is simply exhausting when you can't be yourself. At Lexxic they most definitely practice what they preach, so I would go to work every day and know that I could just be unashamedly myself and share my lived experience to help others. I loved the fact that I could shout about all the incredible things that neurodiverse minds can bring to any working environment. Being a square peg and trying to ram myself in a round hole throughout my career before that was debilitating.'

Georgina firmly believes, as I do, that 'the more we talk about neurodiversity, the more we normalize it and slowly the more we become accepted in society for our unique natures and insights. My mission now is to make the workplace more inclusive for diverse brains, providing an inclusive approach to ensuring everyone is able to understand their own brain; to reduce stigma by sharing my lived experience; and supporting with accredited training for all employees to ensure true neuro-inclusive practices are followed, for the freedom of my clients' employees as human beings.

'I love interacting with individuals who share my passion daily and also interacting with others who understand my own struggles. This makes you feel part of something and truly normal.'

She went on to say that her advice to other individuals with ADHD or dyslexia who feel hindered by their leaders' misconceptions about their neurodiversity, is this: 'Be open, honest and be proud – don't be embarrassed to ask for support if you need it. Having an open honest working relationship with your manager is imperative. When you are able to bring your whole self to work, or you understand yourself fully, that's when you can really start to shine and thrive.'

It's inspiring to hear that although Georgina had to mostly muddle through in the early part of her career, she was able to flip her proactive nature in her favour to switch industries and change her life, first working with Lexxic for over three years and now working with Cognassist. That takes gumption! And it should be applauded. But I also wanted to hear from Georgina what is it that Cognassist do well for their employees that she feels others could replicate when it comes to championing neurodiversity. Because I thought there may be some nuggets of inspiration there for any HR/people leaders reading the book.

'I am proud about the fact that Cognassist regularly go through a diversity, equity and inclusion audit, which has helped us to internally scope out the support needed for all employees, which includes employees with a neuro-difference. We have also set up our own internal employee resource group (ERG), which I have joined, and this includes the development of a peer-to-peer support programme.

'In addition, I present internally and externally on ADHD/dyslexia, raising the profile of neurodiversity and how it impacts individuals and like myself on a personal level in the workplace. All employees at Cognassist have internal neurodiversity training – City and Guilds accredited. The company as a whole encourages open dialogue with supportive managers – which gives staff the ability to communicate their needs, emotional dysregulation and challenges. All employees also take our cognitive assessment when they join the company. It's part of the onboarding process and not specific to those who identify with neurodivergent traits. I took this assessment and believe on a personal level that it has enabled me to get the adjustments and support needed within the Cognassist team to thrive in my role.'

Conclusion

What this detail uncovers when we look at industry leaders like Thriiver, Lexxic and Cognassist is that there are companies, tools and solutions out there that are cost effective, simple to implement and productive in safeguarding and empowering the employees who use them to streamline their working life for the better. So why are most organizations trying to hash their way to a solution off the back of privileged and uninformed leaders?

My advice here is simply to contact one of these organizations and have a chat about what they can do for you based on your size, scale and needs. At least then you have an eye on your business from an objective and expert perspective, and you might actually do some good for your people.

It's very clear to me that championing neurodiversity across businesses both locally and internationally is not only a moral imperative but also a strategic advantage. Companies that embrace neurodiversity unlock the full potential of their workforce, fostering innovation, creativity and a positive workplace culture, as we keep seeing through my exploration in this book. And the foundations for championing neurodiversity involve:

- leadership commitment
- inclusive policies
- collaboration with external organizations
- a continuous focus on learning and adaptation

As companies navigate the complexities of a globalized world, under-standing and embracing neurodiversity becomes integral to sustainable success. The case studies of exemplary companies like JP Morgan Chase, IBM, Santander UK and Google demonstrate the positive impact of neurodiversity initiatives on both on the individuals and across the organizations. And looking at companies like Thriiver, Lexxic and Cognassist, it's clear that overcoming challenges and ensuring long-term success requires a multifaceted approach, including:

• education
• community engagement
• feedback mechanisms
• a holistic perspective on health and wellbeing

So, by championing neurodiversity, companies not only contribute to a more inclusive and equitable society but also position themselves as leaders in the evolving landscape of diversity, innovation and global business excellence.

Don't you want your business to be a part of that revolution?

Notes

1 B Gill. Demystifying neurodiversity: It's time to embrace the different ways we think, JP Morgan Chase & Co, 26 April 2023. www.jpmorganchase.com/news-stories/neurodiversity (archived at https://perma.cc/XWG9-QKDF)

2 IBM. 2023 ESG report: IBM impact, 2023. https://www.ibm.com/impact/files/reports-policies/2023/IBM_2023_ESG_Report.pdf (archived at https://perma.cc/5JW4-J5XX)

3 Santander. Santander and Ambitious about Autism launch new programme to tackle graduate employment, 15 October 2020. www.santander.co.uk/about-santander/media-centre/press-releases/santander-and-ambitious-about-autism-launch-new (archived at https://perma.cc/J5A6-WZH7)

4 American Autism Association. New Google program to hire people with ASD, 17 August 2021. www.myautism.org/news-features/new-google-program-to-hire-people-with-asd (archived at https://perma.cc/SZ59-FWGS)

9

Final thoughts from The Bipolar Businessman

I guess this is the part of the book where the author has to round up what they've learned and send you off into the sunset to take action. And, of course, I will seek to achieve this as best I can. However, before I review what I've learned throughout writing the book and what I hope that businesses can achieve through the inspiration, innovation and best practices presented, it's worth reminding you that it's only through you as an individual that change can take place.

If you trundle off back to your business and the best you can do is stick a few policies in place, then, to all intents and purposes, I have failed you. And I have failed all those within your sphere governance. For it is only in the doing that we achieve. It is only through proactive efforts to shift momentum that we win the day when it comes to wellbeing. Anything less and we will simply continue on the current downward trajectory that we are seeing in businesses the world over.

Throughout my book you will have seen a myriad of evidence to suggest that workplace wellbeing is on the decline, but if you're still not convinced then here are a few takeaways to consider:[1]

- 52% of employees always or often feel exhausted.
- 49% of employee always or often feel stressed.
- 43% of employees always or often feel overwhelmed.
- 34% of employees always or often feel irritable.
- 33% of employees always or often feel lonely.

- 32% of employees always or often feel depressed.
- 27% of employees always or often feel angry.
- Only one-third of the employees that were surveyed reported that their mental and physical health had improved over the last year.

Part of the problem, as I see it, comes down to the inevitable attempts by businesses to strive for a 'blanket bomb' approach to mental health in the workplace. And if my interviews throughout the book are anything to go by then there's a huge demand and need for organizations to start taking a more open and individualized approach to employee wellbeing.

Obviously, the purpose of me writing this book was to focus primarily on neurodivergence and to dive into how embracing neurodiversity can revolutionize your business. However, without a fundamental understanding of where wellbeing as a whole is lacking, or on how we can improve a company landscape when it comes to diversity, equity and inclusion, it's difficult to really get a gauge for where so many problems stem from.

My feeling is that we as human beings are poorly educated when it comes to acceptance and tolerance. We are not given the support we need throughout our formative years to fully understand what mental health means to society, or to us and individuals, and how it might affect the human body. We're also not taught anything about what financial wellbeing means, how to manage money or how to look after ourselves as we breach higher education and move into the world of work. So, how can we be expected to thrive?

The path to change only comes through you, the reader, in your own way. If you're proactive and you acknowledge that it only takes one proactive individual to shape a narrative, then you might come to accept and understand that you can make a difference. The individuals I interviewed during the course of this book were not all blessed with hundreds of staff to execute their success. Most of them stood alone, with good hearts and minds and a want for something better than they were dealt. And, in turn, they've shaped and changed the lives of thousands of people all over the world simply by honouring who they are as individuals and leading by example, on a path that meant something to them.

For the most part, I feel that businesses have forgotten the fundamentals of ethics. Leaders still think that vulnerability is weakness, that people won't follow them, or that they'll get fired if they let people see who they really are. That's an issue that can't be solved unless we seek introspectively to understand who we are as people and what our values are. What inspires you? There's plenty of evidence out there that suggests that we will follow people with passion, vulnerability and purpose. So, anyone who can forge that leadership style into their psyche will win big! But you don't!

I was on stage recently at a major mental health event and someone from the audience asked, 'How can I be a better leader?' and told me that they worked for a very hard company who didn't really look after wellbeing. They told me that their superiors thought that talking about mental health made you weak. I said, 'Firstly talking about mental health doesn't make you weak, it makes you evolved, it means that you recognize that introspection is a value add.' And I told them, 'The problem with senior leaders is that they think being vulnerable means that you have to wash your dirty laundry in public, or that you have to tell people your deepest, darkest fears in order to gain credibility, but this simply isn't the case. Being vulnerable doesn't have to mean that you tell everyone you had a mental breakdown, or that you fought through a tough divorce, or explain to people that someone close to you died. In fact, it doesn't have to be anything that might constitute a lapse in mental health. It could be as simple as talking about a favourite puppy you had when you were a child, because vulnerability isn't about dolling out a sob story, it's simply about affording those around you the ability to see who you are as an individual and what is it about you that evokes some level of human emotion. When you share a part of yourself with someone, they find commonality, irrespective of race, gender, age. They see a little part of who you are as a person and that inspires connection. And the more you are vulnerable with people, the more you realize that they won't run away, and when they don't run away you feel empowered to repeat the process and grow stronger. There may come a time when you do share something with more depth, but it will come from a place of strength and courage, and that's the type of person that people want to follow.'

So. I say, let's start there! Let's consider that you, as a reader, can do more to inspire connection, empathy and change, not only in your business setting but also in your private life – realistically, in every walk of life if you really hone who you are and take the time to consider who you want to be and what impact you want to have in the world then you can become a catalyst for others' evolution and maybe even save some lives along the way.

How embracing neurodiversity can revolutionize your business

And now I come back to the focus of my book. The interviews, studies and learning discussed here, and the knowledge I've tried to impart to you following my 8–10 years working in the wellbeing space, make it clear that embracing neurodiversity can most definitely revolutionize your business. Whether companies take a proactive approach to engaging and understanding their neurodiverse employees is another matter.

It's clear to me that, as with wellbeing generally, the appetite to invest in neurodiversity is still lacking somewhat. Unfortunately, business leaders, C-suite and board directors still need some convincing of the fiscal return on investment. Part of the challenge is that these industry leaders want hard numbers that relate to their fiscal endeavours, but most of the evidence surrounding the development of neurodivergent staff relates to increased productivity, longevity in roles and reduced absenteeism, so with companies having to do their own maths around what that means to the bottom line. They still seem a bit slow on the uptake, even though it's abundantly clear that fewer sick days, better company loyalty and increased productivity will all mean that companies make lots more money.

The Deloitte study that I mentioned in Chapter 7 clearly suggests that what I mentioned above will yield £5 for every £1 you spend on wellbeing in general. And other studies have indicated that, with the right accommodations and support, neurodivergent employees are 30 per cent more productive. I could almost end the book there! That really is the fundamental core of what stakeholders need to wrap their heads around. You will *definitely* make more money if you invest in neurodiversity, and you will *definitely* make more money if you invest in staff wellbeing, diversity, equity and inclusion.

I think my favourite part of writing this book was looking at how eBay do things. Talking to Estelle Jackson, eBay's Global Lead for Diversity, Equity and Inclusion, and deep diving into her values as a human being and how that related to where eBay have completely revolutionized their entire diversity, equity and inclusion processes, policies and practices, it was truly inspiring to see what a company with a budget can do when you have a dynamic, inspiring and value-driven leader running a division whose focus is people. But that, for me, is still an intangible.

What type of leaders does your business have?

There appear to be three types of 'people lead', and by that, I mean three types of individuals who sit in a wellbeing- or people-focused role such as HR, DEI, etc. This is further evidenced based on the people I meet, interview and network with at the biggest wellbeing events around the world.

- **Value-driven:** Firstly, you have the Estelles – these individuals are genuinely and wholeheartedly value-driven. They are inspiring and ethical individuals at their core, and this makes them highly effective and revolutionary when you give them a team and a budget to innovate, as in our eBay example.

- **Award winners:** Secondly you have the award winners. These are the individuals who look and feel like they fit. On paper they look credible – they've got the tenure; they dress nicely and smile at the right time. They sit in a role, looking the part, saying all the right things, but the reins are still held by a bunch of old white men who don't want to upset the status quo. I call these people the award winners because they are seen at face value to be the right fit, they attend events, sit on stage and talk a good game and they win all the awards (that their company usually sponsored in the first place) but they lack the genuine human presence, they lack a level of ethics. It's not to say they don't care but they are often too weak to really speak out. They'd rather talk about their feelings at an event than be sat in the office like Estelle actually doing the work and pushing back on their management to get the job done. But this doesn't move the needle, it's just glorified PR, and the wellbeing industry is littered with them.

- **Stalwarts:** Thirdly there's the stalwarts, those leaders who don't really care either way. They just want a monthly pay check and will keep their mouth shut for fear of reprisal, or, even worse, they are part of the problem, so they hold a role but don't actually believe that change is necessary. They think that the sort of stuff I talk about in this book is fluffy and we shouldn't care about anyone's feelings because it's a work environment and people are just paid to do a job.

Now, the award winners and the stalwarts are clearly damaging to individuals like those I've interviewed and me, who are different. We can even smell their bad energy as soon as we look at them. It's obvious to the neurodiverse whether you have good intent or you're apathetic or lip-service driven, because we thrive off energy. I'm not saying there's not complexity to every human being as an individual, as that would defeat the purpose of my argument. However, it's very obvious to me when I meet the leaders of the big brands who is disingenuous in their endeavours and who is legitimate, and if you ask any of the neurodiverse leaders that I've interviewed they would all say the same. Because we've spent our lives on the sidelines being ostracized for being different, we've not had that much trust for people, so we've had to learn to gauge trust and energy rapidly. That's most certainly a superpower for me. We might not even need to share a sentence and I know whether you're invested in shaking my hand, or if this is a formality so you don't look rude to anyone watching on.

However, the stalwarts will die out. Companies are already getting savvy to the fact that they need the right PR, and if they are a business governed by leaders who can't be bothered, then they will most certainly find themselves an award winner for the post to ensure the PR they need not to have a light shined on them.

The most damaging are the award winners.

The challenge we face currently is that companies are often more interested in building the perception that they are engaged in change, when in reality it's just another fiction. I watched a huge organization I won't name win award after award for maybe eight years. Everything in wellbeing that could be won, their global HR director won, for innovation in wellbeing and beyond, yet in conducting interviews with staff and knowing many who worked at the organization I could clearly see that their wellbeing was not actually moving the needle for anyone. The leader looked like the king of wellbeing, but the staff were unproductive, disenfranchised and consistently unhappy and undervalued, and for me that's the issue that I see as prevalent across many big brands.

Diversity needs to start from the top. We need vulnerable leaders who would inspire you whether they were the company secretary or the CEO. This hiring process needs to come from a place of understanding as to what people gravitate towards. I'd like to see the world of work thriving, with more leaders like Estelle being championed into those roles looking after diversity, because, for me, the 'intangible' that I mentioned comes down to finding those leaders with the innate ability to lead by example and fight for change at the same time. And the intangible means that getting wellbeing right is not sustainable. You might find someone like Estelle and see her in a role like her one at eBay and then see the results, but to replicate that within another organization could be completely impossible without that type of individual in a seat that has enough gravitas and backing to create sustainable change. Until companies focus on the ethics of the individual leading the charge then I fear that wellbeing will continue to decline for most organizations.

How to move the needle for change

There are core factors that I've highlighted throughout the book that come up again and again that could move the needle for change to create an upswing in the context of productivity when it comes to looking after your neurodivergent staff and your wider diverse populace. Here are the highlights that every company should have in place as a *must*:

- **Employee resource groups:** I can't stress enough how much ERGs can change the face of how your company operates. If you are engaged in understanding your various groups of individuals, then give them some weight to inform you of what you need to do. This isn't weak – it's empowering. You will find volunteers across your business who are more than willing to focus on the needs of those with neurodivergent, race-related, gender-related needs and desires. It's your job as a leader to cultivate these minority groups and utilize them to better understand your people and your business.

- **Peer-to-peer support:** Mental health first aiders were a 'nice to have' but they didn't really deliver. Mental health first aid as a certification is a fad in my eyes, and it's been designed to generate revenue off the back of a brand that doesn't really care too much for what's working and cares more about pumping out certification for revenue, than moving the needle. The most effective companies when it comes to wellbeing recognize this issue and focus their efforts on utilizing peer-to-peer support to engage employees and to best serve the needs of their people and those who need support. Ultimately, your peers are those that hold the key to keeping your people safe, so, as with the ERGs, you should be investing in structures surrounding peer-to-peer support if you genuinely want to keep wellbeing on a preventative level and become less reactive as a business.

- **Sensory sensitivities:** Don't underestimate how much impact the senses can have on a neurodiverse employee's overall output. It's easy enough to manage if you look at your individual neurodivergent employees' needs and ask questions. Simple solutions like noise-cancelling headphones, quite spaces and flexible working could be the difference between an individual overloading on a sensory level and suffering issues like burnout or overwhelm that could easily be avoided if you implement some accommodations to help them navigate their working day and their role more effectively, in a way that's right for them.

- **Educate your people:** As with any aspect of wellbeing, you need to implement education. But, as we have seen so far, pretty much every interviewee I spoke to had to self-advocate or even educate those they worked with themselves. And, fundamentally, that's not their job. They have a job, you hired them! So, it's your role as a business or a business leader to bring in speakers, to advocate for the neurodivergent staff and to help implement education across not only your leadership but company-wide, to ensure that your employees understand what neurodiversity is and how to look after those who might identify as neurodivergent. It's too stressful and time-consuming for individuals with neurodiversity to have to educate those they are working with and perform their primary function at the same time. That's not to say that those individuals won't be happy to share their stories, offer insight or advocate. However, your job as an organization should be to implement measures so that they don't have to.

- **Leverage technology and tools:** Careful delineation as to what technology you should use, whether that be software, hardware, apps, employee assistance programmes or beyond, is paramount to a sustainable support mechanism. The priority for me is always to be human first, but you must understand how to capitalize on the technology that's out there to best support the needs of your staff, especially the neurodivergent. Forget about the fancy, shiny apps that go in and out of fashion, because you often spend money unnecessarily and get limited engagement. However, if you empower your ERGs to define the technology that works for them you can make more educated decisions about what you invest your budget in, and you know that those individuals are focused on what will bring value for them. Taking a sudden liking to this piece of tech, or that app, in a boardroom because one of the execs knows the founder, or saw it in the *FT*, is not a sustainable way to spend your money. Ask your people, hear what they have to say and empower them to help you make informed decisions.

- **Leadership commitment:** Get your senior leaders to commit to neurodiversity, through everything from inclusive hiring practices, to mentorship, advocacy, awareness and the implementation of those points I mentioned above, and you *will* move the needle! Those companies who have management 'buy-in' are already moving far faster towards sustainable change for their neurodiverse people than those companies who only have a little bit of people- or HR-led support. If the directors are invested, budgets will be found, lives will be changed, and your value structure will be more aligned with your people's needs. Without a true and legitimate leadership commitment, your company will undoubtedly fail to evolve, and people who are neurodiverse will simply leave you to work for those who will best look after their needs.

There are so many aspects when it comes to embracing neurodiversity, and indeed the wider diverse needs of your employees, that I could write you lists all day long, but the above are the core things that need to be done if you want to set a steady foundation.

That being said, I leave this book where my story began in saying that everything you do is about people. Stop thinking about money, key performance indicators or the company directive. You will get everything you desire if you focus on people.

I've shown you examples of neurodivergent individuals thriving, whether that be through their own businesses/initiatives, or as part of a big brand; I've shown you companies that are growing their profits year on year because they invest more in their employees and the diversity that is to be cherished within any organization; I've even shown you which companies are innovating and leading their industries because they are specifically investing in people with neurodiversity. The evidence is overwhelmingly substantial, and the results are obvious to anyone with their eyes open.

Your choice when you finish reading this book is simply to decide what kind of person you want to be. What kind of impact do you want to have on those around you? Not just in the office, but when you walk down the street. When you see someone having a panic attack in the shops, will you walk away?

We all make choices every day, whether to turn a blind eye, or to engage in life and the individuals that envelop our sphere of energy. Our common misconception is that our voice doesn't matter, but we are wrong. You as an individual, regardless of your rank or vocation, your seniority or sway, you can make a difference. You can change a life! Stop concerning yourself with whether you might miss out because you spoke up and start focusing more readily on what is the right thing to do. I promise you that you will never regret letting your voice be heard, if there's honour and intent in what you wish to say.

As a neurodivergent individual myself, I never wanted to be treated differently in the workplace – I simply wanted to be heard. I wanted people to cherish who I was and how unique I was, and during those moments where I had leaders who understood my value I felt most whole internally, and I would have gone to the trenches to deliver for them; I still do in many instances.

When you strive to understand someone as complex as those with neurodiversity, it's not something we forget, because very often you might be one of the few who ever bothered to sit and listen. For some, maybe you're the first person who ever cared to listen and understand us. And when you spend your life being told you're different, or naughty, or loud, or that you don't do things the way they've always been done, then you either clam up and try to mask who you are or, if you're lucky, you find someone who might empathize or see the beauty in your innovative mind.

Let us remind ourselves that most of human achievement came off the back of individuals thinking differently about how to do things. Let us educate ourselves and care about those who are diverse and unique in the way they approach the world. Let us see the beauty in those that may find nuances to a problem we never knew was there. Let us humble ourselves through the innovations of others.

I believe that if we afford ourselves the awareness that, historically, the whole of humanity and our planet has evolved more rapidly because of the diverse nature of our connections, our trade, our learning and sharing of knowledge, our love and global community, and that this has led to us becoming a hugely advanced and unique civilization in so many ways, then perhaps we might better understand why we need to get back to that.

The world has become a very divisive place in recent years, but if you are open-minded, humble and adaptive, and if at the crux of your core values you value love and kindness and fundamental ethics above a want for building your ego through self-grandiosity or greed, then you can truly become part of a wider movement that's changing the way we live and cherishes those alongside you that tread this life with us toward forging the brighter future we all seek as human beings. So, lets strive for that and succeed together!

Note

1   S Torkington. Wellbeing and mental health, World Economic Forum, 23 June 2023. www.weforum.org/agenda/2023/06/workplace-well-being-declining-health/ (archived at https://perma.cc/BQU6-CG8K)

INDEX

Looking for another book?

Explore our award-winning
books from global business
experts in Responsible
Business

Scan the code to browse

www.koganpage.com/responsible-
business

Also available

ISBN: 9781398600249

www.koganpage.com

THIS PAGE IS INTENTIONALLY LEFT BLANK

From 4 December 2025 the EU Responsible Person (GPSR) is:
eucomply oÜ, Pärnu mnt. 139b – 14, 11317 Tallinn, Estonia
www.eucompliancepartner.com

www.ingramcontent.com/pod-product-compliance
Lightning Source LLC
Chambersburg PA
CBHW071555210326
41597CB00019B/3258